The Socialist International
at Gunpoint

Other titles by Manos Haris:

'Nikos Kazantzakis commemorative album', Difros Publications, sponsored by the Municipal Authorities of Heraklion, Crete, Athens 1981.

'In the Constellation of Cobra', Line Publications, Athens 1980.

'Minotaurus Blood' - Symbolic diary, Athens 1981.

'Military bases, NATO and PASOK - Andrea you are the first who said that' Truth Publications, Athens 1983.

'Terrorism - first daughter of CIA', G. Ladias Publications, Athens, 1984.

'Terrorism' translated into Bulgarian, Patriotic Front Publications, Sofia, 1985.

'Terrorism' translated into Russian, Novosti-APN Publications, Moscow, 1985.

'Terrorism' translated into English, Dorriston Publications, London, 1985.

'The Pentagon of Death', G. Ladias Publications, Athens, 1986.

THE SOCIALIST INTERNATIONAL AT GUNPOINT

MANOS HARIS

translated from the Greek by
CONSTANTINE MAKROPOULOS

Photoset and printed in Great Britain by
Picton Print, Citadel Works,
Chippenham, Wiltshire.

This book is dedicated to the memory of my unforgotten friend and comrade in arms Petros Vavalis, an honest, conscientious, pure, invincible and original socialist, who, through his multifaceted activities, has contributed greatly to the war against the dark forces, mainly from his position as President of the Committee of Mediterrean Solidarity, but also in the attempt to solve the problems of the 3rd world.

ΜΑΝΟΣ ΧΑΡΗΣ

Η Σοσιαλιστική Διεθνής στο στόχαστρο της CIA

ΕΚΔΟΣΕΙΣ Γ. ΛΑΔΙΑΣ – ΑΘΗΝΑ 1986

Cover of the Greek Edition designed by Michael Nicolinacos.

viii

A red rose for Olaf Palme,
murdered by the enemies of
Socialism and Peace

Olaf Palme, the Swedish Socialist leader, the second victim in a row after Indira Gandhi, member of the 'Group of Six' which is struggling against the nuclear arms race and for the establishment of peace in the world. For those reasons its members have always been a target of the CIA.

Contents

Dedication to Petros Vavalis vii
Dedication to Olaf Palme xii
Preface – *Vassos Mathiopoulos* ix
A Red Rose for Olaf Palme xiv
1   Olaf Palme and his Loss 1
2   Introduction to the Subject of the Book 4
3   A Different Opinion Regarding Socialist International 17
4   The Last Convention of Socialist International in Lima? Peru was 'Awash with Blood' 23
5   Willy Brandt's curriculum vitae 28
6   The opening speech of the convention of Socialist International in Lima 33
7   Lima's Manifest at the Convention of Socialist International June 20-30, 1986 42
8   A Confidential Report about Socialist International made at the expense of the CIA 58
9   The Positions of S.I. and the Displeasure of the United States 74
10 French Socialists Under the Pressure of the U.S. 90
11 The U.S.A. and the British Library Party 97
12 North European Countries Under American Fire 100
13 CIA's International Campaign of Defamation against Andreas Papandreou PASOK and Greece 117
14 Pasok and Papandreou are under attack, by their former Party's Officials 133
    Epilogue 137

Willy Brandt who as the President of Socialist International contributed greatly
to world peace.

Preface

The Socialist International constitutes the most solid and enduringly consistent rallying point of progressive forces in our times. Being a continuation of the Second International, which sprang from the International Workingmen's Association (established in 1864 in London), it exerts considerable influence in contemporary international politics. With member-countries in Europe, Asia, Latin America and Africa, it has acquired the international prestige that enables it to play a decisive role in the context of rapprochement between East and West, in the development of the south striving to achieve the socio-economic development of the north and in the crucial issue of disarmament.

It has acquired additional prestige since, 14 years ago, Willy Brandt was elected as its president, enhancing it with his personality and energy. Apart from boosting the presence of Third World countries as members, the Socialist International continued to pursue a policy of goodwill towards the East, a policy which had been initiated by Willy Brandt during his Chancellorship of the Federal Republic of Germany, and reasserted its views on world detente. Equally pioneering was its approach of bringing together the socialist and communist parties – the Italian and Yugoslav Communist Parties and more recently others. This, in the era of perestroika, is heralding a profound reordering of social evolution as a whole, with year 2000 in perspective, and a gradual return to the roots of both world movements in the framework of modern political reality: a social and democratic policy with personal freedom, human dignity and the total abolition of exploitation of man by man at its heart.

It was natural that this course, which an International of working people chose to take in every sector of life, would provoke the powers of reaction, still all-powerful in the world, that had hoped to be able to bring the Socialist International under their own control.

Manos Haris's book – the author is a crusader in the struggle for equal opportunities – is both timely and revealing. Based on the tragic experience of the colonels' military dictatorship of 1967–1974, Manos Haris exposes the ruthless war waged by the powers of decadence and retrogression against the Socialist International. The evidence he presents evokes in his reader a particular interest as well as abhorrence concerning the methods employed by the paragons of the 'Black International' intent to slander and nullify the ideas for which the great founders of the enlightenment and the social revolutionaries fought; the same ideals that are now being transformed into action by the Socialist International everywhere. In this sense the author renders international journalism a valuable service and contributes to exposing fanatic enemies of peace and social progress.

This year the 125th anniversary of the foundation of the German Social-Democratic Party by Lassal (the oldest genuine Socialist Party in Europe) is being celebrated. Willy Brandt, its leader for 23 years and now its honorary chairman, is aware of the forthcoming publication of this book by Manos Haris, and is looking forward to reading it and expressing his valued opinion.

In a time of confusion and disorientation books like Manos Haris's contribute to the clarification of what is really going on in the wider international political scene. The author set out to write his book with boldness and meticulousness and has succeeded in producing a useful report which should be valued and appreciated accordingly.

V. P. Mathiopoulos

A Red Rose for Olaf Palme

The red rose has become, internationally, a symbol of love. In Sweden, though, the red rose also symbolizes the sympathy, the compassion, the political struggle for equal rights. It is the symbol of the Swedish Social Party, which had, as a leader, the unforgettable Olaf Palme, who was killed following Indira Gandhi's murder, at the armed hand of a paid killer. It is no secret who pays the killers. Not of course the Socialists and the Peacemakers. It is rather obvious that they are people whose massive, murderous plans are hatched in the dark centres of Imperialism and Zionism, plans which are executed in cold blood by secret agencies like CIA and MOSSAD – people who are troubled by the activities of the defenders of Socialism and Peace.

If we remember for a moment what surprising things Olaf Palme has done for freedom, equality of rights, indeed for the whole planet, then we can easily conclude who were the murderers of this peace carrying dove.

Palme was the man who took charge of the campaign against Racism, having as its symbol an outspread hand, under which it reads: 'Leave my brother in peace'.

During the Vietnam War, Olaf Palme was the first who came on to the streets of Stockholm, protesting against the American raid, waking up the sleeping conciousness of the people.

He was a champion in the struggle for the independence of his nation and the world in general. He was the deciding factor in the acceptance of the Independence Party of Puerto Rico as a member of Socialist International, in which Palme was a leading force.

Palme was an unshakeable rock in the case of Nicaragua, supporting the revolution with all his heart, giving generously of emotional and material help, standing firm against enormous pressures. No other leader was so generous in material and human help towards the nations of the Third World.

Palme helped, more than anybody else, Andreas Papandreou, during his struggle against the American motivated, Greek military Junta of 1967.

Palme was a negotiator in the neglected bloody war between Iran-Iraq, where thousands of lives have, and are still, being lost.

He was the leader concerned about all the unsolved problems, defending whoever suffered. Any injustice made him angry, but his anger was never displayed politically.

Whenever Palme was fighting for humanistic ideals, he always displayed humane attitudes, as has been said characteristically about him by Robin Martinez, President of the Independent Party of Puerto Rico. Xavier Peroz de Gueyar also said that 'Palme was a man who fought for peace using only virtues'.

His successor, the new Swedish Prime Minister Carrison said:

'Death is at the same time a reminder for life. Olaf Palme's life is explicit proof that a life can be a gleaming smile with an infinite value'.

Together with Palme's successor and the King of Sweden, who paid their respects on behalf of the Swedish nation, was the General Secretary of the United Nations. Mr Xavier Perez de Gueyar, the Prime Minister of India, Mr. Gandhi, and the President of Socialist International, Mr. Willy Brandt, who all expressed the sorrow of the whole world. They spoke on behalf of President Mitterrand of France, Kohl of Germany, Gonzales of Spain, Papandreou of Greece, Craxi of Italy, Soares of Portugal, Ortega of Nicaragua, Kaunda of Zambia, as well as the hundreds of millions who were not present at the funeral – those about whom Palme used to say:

'the people who have no voice'.

The huge and brilliant international political figure of Palme was the reason that personalities like the leader of Lebanon, Jumblat, the Prime Minister of Israel, Peres, Kohl of W. Germany, Honeker of DDR and Rizkov, the Prime Minister of USSR were present at the funeral.

Many others paid their respects, although the unforgettable and renowned Socialist had been their adversary. It is known that for many years, U.S. Governments refused to invite Palme, though he was leader of the Swedish nation, because of his anti-imperialistic position. Even so the U.S. sent their Minister of Foreign Affairs, Mr Schultz. It was a gesture reminiscent of an old custom of the Mafia, who sent the biggest and most spectacular funeral wreaths to their murdered victims and came to console his relatives in person!

Puerto Rican, Robert Martinez, dedicating an article with the title 'A red rose for Olaf Palme' wrote characteristically:

'If the assassin had had the opportunity to know Palme personally as his many friends knew him, he would never have committed such a crime'.

For all these reasons, Swedish people who knew Palme well, threw thousands of red roses during the funeral procession in Stockholm, thus changing that cold winter day of his funeral, Saturday 15th March, 1986, to a spring day. They also created in every Swedish home a modest little 'sanctuary' with Palme's photograph, a white candle and a red rose.

In that simple and modest way, Swedish people paid their respect to their fellow man, their Prime Minister, the original Socialist, the leader with the 'sweet smile and clear eyes', who showed to the world through his actions that a small country can be an example and a source of inspiration of humanity, and who also reminded the supreme powers that power without justice and humanism can never gain the love and devotion of the people.

Let this chapter, written instead of a preface to this book, be another 'red rose' for Olaf Palme, the selected member of Socialist International, who made, through his death, a great sacrifice to humanity. He makes us understand that though the altars built of red roses may cause sorrow to people who make them in honour of heroes like Palme, they also encourage their spirits to continue the fair battle against dark forces.

The red roses are to honour the people who fight for the benefit of humanity, their stems are to strike symbolically the patrons of murderers like those who are embodied by the CIA.

Manos Haris

1
Olaf Palme and his Loss

Olaf Palme was born on 30 January 1927. He was the youngest of an aristocratic family with three children. Although his health was not good he was early fond of learning.

In his fourth year, he could speak German and French as well as his mother tongue. His precocious abilities were developed in private schools for the privileged. After his term of service in the army Palme was promoted to the rank of sub-lieutenant of cavalry. Later on, he obtained a scholarship to Canyon College in Ohio. He graduated, in 1948, with a scientific degree. The following year he married a Czechoslovak student who wanted to defect to the West. Following their return to Sweden, they got divorced, as had previously been planned. In 1950 Palme joined the Social Democratic Labour Party. At the same time he was awarded a law degree at the University of Stockholm.

He became Vice President of Socialist International and a member of the Independent Committee for International Cooperation of the ex-chancellor of W. Germany, Willy Brandt – a committee which dealt with problems and relations between the rich North and the poor South.

The Swedish leader laid the foundations for, and then lead, the committee known as 'Palme Committee', which in 1982 submitted to the General Congress of the U.N. a proposal regarding International Security, something which was greatly appreciated by the General Secretary of U.N., Mr. Gueyar. Palme was beloved by Western supporters of constructive dialogue with the East, because he defended proposals to declare Northern and Central Europe a nuclear weapons free zone.

The assassination of Palme ended the life of Sweden's greatest political figure, the most respected defender of disarmament and Democratic Socialism. This violent action put an end to a political career which covered more than 30 years, leading the Swedish Socialdemocratic Party for the second time since September 1986.

Outside his native Scandinavia, Palme's name was heard for the first time in the 60's when he courageously denounced the U.S. involvement in the Vietnam War. In 1968, being then Minister of Education, he came down in the streets to take part in an anti-American demonstration on the side of

Vietnam's Ambassador. This behaviour infuriated the American Government, while the Swedish opposition parties asked for his resignation. One year later he became Prime Minister of Sweden.

Olaf Palme himself once said: 'I was born into the aristocracy but I belong to the labour class. I joined the movement for freedom, equal rights and brotherhood between people'.

Palme's Party lost the parliamentary elections in 1976, but they won again in 1982 and formed a Government. His political support for a new international economic order and his opposition to the expanded militarization of Earth and Space gave much concern to the warlike minded 'hawks' of Washington, who were relying on their dogma of 'National Security'. The Declaration of Delhi, bearing the signatures of five leaders (Sweden, India, Greece, Tanzania and Mexico) and also his appeal for restraint in the arms race, was distasteful to these 'hawks'. The position of the Swedish Government towards European affairs was many times a disappointment to the U.S. authorities.

George Bush, ex-Director of CIA and now Vice President of the USA refused to agree with any of the legislative committees on the subject of condemnation of political assassinations, citing as an excuse 'National Security'. In the beginning of the 60's plans for political assassinations were an integral part of the foreign policy of Washington. The present U.S. Government threw away any pretence and it now appears to some to be the organiser of terrorism and other criminal activities around the world.

A respectable Mexican newspaper 'Exelsior' quotes an article written by Leon Roberto Garcia, a Mexican reporter, '...We think that the assassination of Olaf Palme is shameful...We need to put an end to CIA's murders. The world cannot live under the threat of nuclear terrorism as it is applied by the Ministry of Foreign Affairs and President Reagan'.

Another reporter named Frida Modak from 'DIA' newspaper writes: 'Palme's assassins were terrorists, the kind of people who try to find an excuse for their warlike policy by using the pretence of 'anti-terrorism'. We must remember that when Orlando, ex Minister of Chile was murdered, the organizers of that assassination were also planning an attack against other political people. Among the organizers was the American Townlee, an agent of the Chilian terrorist group DINA, thought to be a branch of the CIA.

One of the political figures, whom they were planning to kill when he visited Madrid, was Olaf Palme. That plan, though, was not then successful.

According to western political observers, Palme's assassination was meant to frustrate his election as President of Socialist International, which event could prove to be a big stumbling block to American policy. The

2

names of Papandreou and Gonzales were often mentioned as possible successors of Willy Brandt. To the Americans though, both candidates were unacceptable. The likeliest possibility is Brynland, Prime Minister of Norway, because the Socialist Party led by her has a lot of influence in the USA. Some people also say that her husband, (who is a known member of the Conservative Party) is cooperating at a high level with the CIA.

The Prime Minister of Greece Andreas Papandreou (left) with Olaf Palme soon to be murdered.

2

Introduction to the Subject of the Book

The main theme of the book is the secret war between American Imperialism and International Zionism on the one hand, and Socialist International plus all the Socialdemocratic Parties or Governments, mainly of Western Europe, on the other.

These dark forces of Imperialism recognize that Socialism is possibly gaining ground and that the countries of Western Europe are slowly but steadily under different types of socialism or socialdemocracy departing from the so-called western influence. Of course imperialists react as strongly as they can. They do not understand, and they do not want to believe, that the nations are about to take a major step towards a true and fair Socialism.

They are trying to strike at Socialist International and Governments or parties with a socialist trend through their agents, mainly of the CIA.

Europe, especially Western Europe, is a territory of special importance for American Imperialism, firstly because the USA needs to be assured of a passage to the Middle East and Arab countries, and secondly because Europe will become a great power following its projected union, something that the USA wishes to avoid. Thus the USA tries to expel Socialism in order that European Governments can be controllable as in the past. After all, Europe being close to the USSR, a country of existing socialism, causes the USA concern from a strategic point of view. What is going to happen in a state of war or general competition if America's rival, the USSR try to break the ties and deflect the obedience of NATO's members from the USA?

America thus, heeding political changes and looking far to the future (we have Vietnam as an example) try not to lose any time. Through a network of spies and secret agents they become involved with and try to infiltrate any movement, party or government which they suspect of socialist trends.

If they lose the game of influence in a country, they will lose a great deal: their expansionism, the military bases and strategic points around the world from where they launch their great plans sometimes reaching even beyond earth limits to the stars (for example ambitious Star War Project).

4

This book, written by a Greek author, examines the case of Greece, pointing out how the USA has been involved and continues to act through the CIA against the Greek Socialist Party (PASOK), its Government and Andreas Papandreou himself.

Preliminarily I must point out the case of the ex-congressman and member of PASOK, Demos Botsaris, who in conjunction with some other associates of Papandreou, turned out to be the most malicious amongst Papandreou enemies, making public declarations, writing books and publishing articles in newspapers. There is also the case of Arsenis who had maintained old ties with the USA; and the case of Alexakis, the ex-chief of the Greek Secret Service Branch (former KYP and now EYP) who although being under the direct control of Papandreou, found a way to maintain a 'routine' cooperation with the CIA as was proven when the case of the double-agent Krystallis came to the light.

Another remarkable case is that of the Soviet Bochan, a KGB man who defected from Greece to the USA, with the help of the CIA and who revealed that he had supposedly, in cooperation with Greek associates, been misleading the Greek authorities into believing that the USSR were spying against Greece, in spite of the fact that both countries were developing good relations. This was a diplomatic distortion of facts against Papandreou and it happened just before the scheduled meeting of the Greek Prime Minister Papandreou with Reagan to discuss the matter of military bases. The CIA reasoning was that Papandreou, having in mind Soviet espionage, would change his previous decision to do away with the American bases of death and the nuclear weapons existing in our country.

USA intentions are also to neutralize Turkey's rival, Bulgaria, which has been proven a good friend and neighbour of Greece, so that in the event of war with Turkey, Cyprus or Greece it will be ensured that Bulgaria will not assist Greece. That's why the USA cited amongst other names supposedly involved in the Soviet espionage against Greece, the Bulgarians S. Sevdalov, V. Mitrovski, B. Gonkov, K. Petrov and B. Asparouhov.

Fortunately though, Papandreou, known for his clever diplomacy abroad – despite the machinations of those inside the country – was not caught in the CIA trap and during his last visit to Sofia he co-signed a treaty of friendship which will be of great importance if Turkey decides to move against Greece in the future.

Subsequently in this book the activities of the CIA against other countries are revealed and the reasons why the USA fights against Socialist International are explained. It must be clear from the beginning that the most important reasons why Socialist International is threatened by the

CIA are the following:

1. The ability of Socialist International to stop the nuclear weapons race.
2. The increasing reputation of Socialist International among the popular anti war associations in various countries as people increasingly desire peace.
3. Socialist International has not only the potentital for action but also a wide ideological aspect, which is unfortunately not yet full realised.

Other points defining the opposition between the USA and Socialist International, explaining the controversy between them are the following:

– There are many examples of American feelings against Socialist International and the Socialist parties of Europe and the Balkans such as: the refusal of Reagan to meet Willy Brandt, the respects paid by Reagan to the SS Cemetery and also the support given by sections of the USA to all the conservative parties which assist the militarism of US policy.

– The struggle against the nuclear weapons race and the so called Star Wars.

– The attention paid recently by the USA to the European Socialist Parties which they can no longer ignore.

– The refusal of the representatives of the Socialist Parties of the member countries of NATO at the Lisbon Conference to discuss the matter of the establishment of American missiles in Europe, because each of them had adopted a different attitude to that subject.

– The fact that the situation in Europe became more complicated after the establishment of American warheads and the Soviet counter-measures.

– the contractive proposals of Socialist International at the Press Conference in Geneva and the initiatives they took in trying to find a common ground for discussion between the two Super Powers, USA and USSR.

– The fact of the unacceptable demand of the USA to establish the warhead missiles Pershing and Cruise in Holland, which was refused by Holland to the satisfaction of the people.

One more basic reason for their attitude against Socialist International is the fact that the latter, under the strong leadership of Willy Brandt, reveals to the world the dangers to humanity of the plans carefully prepared by the 'falcons' of Zionism, who really govern America. Specifically, Socialist International reveals the suspicious role the USA plays in international terrorism, which is controlled with such dexterity by the mighty CIA in order to promote the plans of Imperialism and Zionism.

On July 1985 under the domes of Constitution Hall in Washington, President Reagan spoke to the American Law Union, showing to the whole world the hypocritical role played by 'Government of Republicans' towards the problem of terrorism. Previously the boss of the White House had made an appeal to the terrorists of Angola, Afghanistan, Laos and Nicaragua who had been gathered in one of the camps of UNITA, under the flag of Democrat International, created by the USA as a counter-weight to Socialist International. In addition to this, Reagan personally promoted terrorism as a matter of governmental policy, signing in April 1984 the top secret directive 138, by which he allowed acts of diversion on the ground of third world countries, under the pretence of fighting against terrorism. In reality, directive 138 allows the CIA, Pentagon and other Services of the USA to plan and execute secret terrorist acts against governments whose policy does not comply with the interests of USA.

According to the extensive programme of the USA government, CIA is responsible for the training of saboteur and terrorist gangs in more than twelve countries around the world like Honduras, Guatemala, Israel, Costa Rica, Pakistan, Paraguay, Salvador, Turkey etc. One of the main aims of CIA in Central American is to provide help of any kind to the anti-Nicaraguan government of Contras in order to cause conflict and trouble on the Nicaraguan borders, as well as other terrorist activities, and in this way to destabilize the country.

The training of saboteurs and the support of Contras against the Nicaraguan government is a brainchild of William Casey, the well known Head of CIA. Casey's enthusiasm for operations like the above was such that he personally visited Honduras many times in order to inspect how the saboteur groups operate and to supply their needs. CIA printed a guide which was distributed freely among the Contras and which could create a scandal with the instructions openly suggesting to them, among other things such acts as sabotage against the Santinistas movement and anyone else who could put obstacles in the way of the execution of the 'secret CIA operations'. The guide advises guerillas to punish in public the officials of Santinistas and to organise, secretly, assassinations against their own associates, presenting them as victims of the factory of Santinistas, to black mail ordinary citizens in neighbouring countries around Nicaragua, into helping the counter-revolutionists. The guide includes over 40 pictures of industrial installations. The destruction of these sites could paralyze the normal life of Nicaragua.

The mercenaries among the saboteurs, who's task is to get involved in the interior affairs of a country, are recruited as agents of CIA from among the immigrants who come for different reasons to the USA. The 'procurers' of CIA do not have any moral hesitation in recruiting even criminals who are serving a prison term. The selection is based on the principle of 'no questions

7

asked'. They are taken out of prison, given money, new identification cards, passport and fake C.V. in exchange for a guarantee to obey even the most monstrous orders. The officials of the special services of USA prefer to recruit mercenaries from among the immigrants and the common criminals, because they can easily get rid of them if they need to. The recruitment of such terrorists is made easy by the help of private organisations existing and operating in USA.

At present there are in operation about 25 camps and 130 private schools for the training of terrorists in over 10 States of the USA. In Alabama forests, in Colorado mountains, in Arizona and Nevada deserts the so-called 'Wild Geese' are in training. The best equipped special training centres for the preparation of saboteurs and terrorist groups are in the U.S. Army bases in Fort Bragg, North Carolina, Fort Benning, Georgia, Fort Levis, Washington State, Fort Shilla, Oklahoma, Fort Scott, Kansas and Trinidad in Colorado. Particularly in Trinidad, north of Baton City, on the borders of Colorado with New Mexico, 500–800 mercenaries are in training at any one time under the guidance of 30 trainers. One can find there mainly immigrants from Latin America (Honduras, Guatemala, Nicaragua, Salvador). The future mercenaries are trained in shooting with different kinds of weapons, in sabotage, in developing dexterity in the use of toxic weapons, in orientating themselves in the darkness of the night etc.

In Fort Scott camp, south of Topec City, Kansas, a compound saboteur training program takes place with terrorists recruited from among Cuban exiles, and immigrants from Argentina, Grenada, Peru and Uruguay. In Shilla camp, north of Lowton Town, Oklahoma, Latin Americans are in training and also men who come from Asia and Africa. Near Birmingham, Alabama, there is 'Ronda', a private school for saboteur training, where in exchange for $350 they will teach you how to kill a man with a knife or bare hands, how to use fire arms and explosives etc in a programme which lasts 2 weeks. The owner of the school, Franklin Camber, a Vietnam Veteran, does not hide his connections with the special services of the USA. In this school, Sikh terrorists, who were responsible for the deaths of 329 passengers on the Air India plane which was exploded on 23-6-1985 over the Atlantic Ocean and for the explosion of a bomb in the luggage department of the Norit Airport in Tokyo, were trained. Considering all these facts a reasonable question may arise: Isn't it really hypocritical when the U.S. Government accuses of international terrorism other countries which reject American imposition? The officials of the USA close their eyes to the network of schools which undertake the training of mercenaries and assassins inside their own country. The activity of the CIA and the U.S. Pentagon in such operations as the training of terrorists and their use in the undeclared war against the people of Asia, Africa and Latin America is illegal according to article. 18 of the Organization Charter of the United Nations, reading that no country or group of countries will have the right to be involved either directly or indirectly in the interior affairs of another country. This article prohibits not only armed, but any form of involvement or threat against the integrity of a country, or the political, economical and cultural elements of the same.

It must be pointed out that officials of Reagan's administration do not really hide the terrorist intentions of the USA. In July 1985 the State Department Secretary, Schultz, declared in San Francisco that the USA has a moral obligation to assist in the removal of legal, but undesirable to the USA, governments of independent countries. As regards Nicaragua, it has been said that this case requires immediate action on the part of the USA. Recently similar threats had been made against Muarmar Kadhafi, the leader of Libya. Declarations of that kind from an official representative of the USA are directly opposed to the resolution of the General Assembly of the United Nations for the elimination of state terrorism, or other similar activities, on the part of countries intending to undermine the social-political institutions of other dominant countries.

Although that is the real situation, the USA have the impudence to accuse other countries, including recently Greece, of terrorist activities while, according to the denunciations of Socialist International, it is proven that the USA have a long history of terrorism. Since the establishment of the United States, terrorism has been used by some individuals or organisations for the implementation of particular purposes. In present days the government of the USA employs terrorism as a tool of state policy and a means to solve serious strategic or international problems. In the 60's and 70's an average of 100 terrorist incidents per decade have occurred, 31 incidents in 1982, 51 incidents in 1983 and 8 incidents in 1984, seven of which were bomb attempts inside New York. In 1984 the most active terrorist group was 'United Front for Freedom' which had been unknown until that time and was not completely unmasked, because its activity ceased as suddenly as it had started.

In such terrorist activity, but in a racist way, some extreme right wing nazi groups like the Klu Klux Klan and especially the 'Long Knives' are employed. The most active extreme right wing terrorist groups are: 'Order', 'White American Fortress', 'Silent Brotherhood'. 'Aryan Nations', 'American Nazi Party'. These groups are neo-nazi organisations, small in numbers but very well organised, with adequate weapons and financial means. Some of their leaders are not so much fanatic ideologists but are motivated by money or for personal benefit, that's why they are using their groups mainly for bank robberies. The leader of 'Order', between 1983–84, by robbing banks, insurance companies and post offices made over 4.5 million dollars! The group was outlawed after the murder of a government official and a member of the National Guard.

We must point out that in the USA there is no law that prohibits the organisation of a neo-nazi group which is perfectly legitimate but in practice all these groups and organisation are closely watched by the Counter Intelligence Service. All neo-nazi groups are being watched by 'Bnie Bate Society' which informs both the public and counterintelligence services who act accordingly.

The group 'Order' has about 100 members. The leader is Bruce Caroll Pierce. 'Order' originates from another nazi group, 'Aryan Nations' with Richard Butler as leader. 'Order' has recruited the most aggressive members of the racist movement. It gets protection from the Police. There are some suspicians that the Counter Intelligence Service know 'Orders' hideaways and shelters but is not in a hurry to clear up the gang). They just strike from time to time.

The most numerous and active white terrorist group the so-called 'Aryan Nations', has 500 members. Its headquarters are in Nineteen, Lake of Idaho. This organisation's strategy, though, is milder, in spite of the declaration of war they have made against those occupied by Zionists government.

The recruiting of their members involves a 'points system'. In order to became a hero and qualify automatically to become a member of 'Aryan Nations' one must kill a black, a Jew or a judge or other official person. However a person can also qualify to become a member by doing less major criminal acts such as assault or robbery. There are close relations between the nazi groups and Klu Klux Klan. For example, Lewis Beam, the former leader of KKK in Texas is now responsible for the modern system of communication with computers between the 'Aryan Nations' and the other right wing extremist groups.

Police have arrested right wing terrorists who belong to nazi groups in the states of Washington, Montana, California, Idaho, Oregon, Florida, N. Mexico, North Carolina, Georgia and Alabama. In reality these arrests cover the geographical borders of right wing racist groups in the USA.

The activity of the KKK has been reduced in Florida, Tennessee and Texas, but is somehow, picking up in Georgia and North Carolina. Some KKK groups exist in Kentucky, Maryland, Pennsylvania, West Virginia, N. Jersey and N. York (about 300,000 members). In middle Western States

KKK groups are in Illinois, two of them in Kentucky, three in Ohio, three in Missouri and three smaller groups in Indiana.

On 3 April 1985 the Chief of the counterintelligence service announced to the Subcommittee of the Senate for Security and Terrorism that 'the right wing terrorist groups show significant aptitudes towards violence... They are more dangerous and stronger than the old groups of KKK from which the new ones are drawn'. Their dogma is racial and religious hatred, they have large stocks of weapons, strong protectors in Police and Government Offices and they are hiding usually in thinly inhabited areas of the country. In the right wing groups we should also mention 'Islamic Nation' which represents a religious section of Back Muslims under the leadership; of Lewis Farahan and declares the superiority of the black race. During the past 2–3 years it was not accused of any criminal activity, despite the sharp and explicit language of their bombastic leader.

There is a series of other organisations with a nationalist character, which are employed in terrorist activity. Some of them like the self-exiled Cuban's group, work with the American Special Services blessing and guidance. The Puerto-Rican National group has a loose organisation and they are under surveillance by the police. The life of this group is short and their actions non significant, restricted geographically to areas of large Puerto-Rican population, because Police officers entered into the group's ranks. The restriction inside the States though, does not exclude terrorist activity abroad, with the exclusion of U.S. citizens only. The same thing happens in the case of American nationalist organisation and especially ASALA (American Secret Army for Liberation of America).

In reaction to the frequent occurrence of terrorist incidents against American citizens abroad, the government spent 100 million dollars in 1983 and almost 200 million dollars in 1984 for the safeguarding and protection of Embassies and in building up fences, warning and other defensive systems around American military bases and other installations.

We must point out that in 1984 there were 77,032 American citizens, officials or people cooperating with the U.S. services, military men, people travelling as tourists, commercial represenatives etc., who were protected by American authorities. The counter-intelligence service of the USA and mainly the CIA has since 1983 started a public awareness program in matters of security and defence against terrorist actions through which they keep informed all the American representatives abroad.

President Reagan on 3 April 1984 signed directive no. 138 by which various instructions were given preventing terrorism even to the extent of planning retaliatory measures and preventive strikes against terrorist groups, which were threatening the lives of American citizens' inside the USA and abroad. The measures which have been taken inside the country are the following:

1) Improvement in the guarding of the White House, the State Dept, the U.S. delegate in the United Nations in New York etc. For this purpose the following has been done: fencing organisation and use of trained dogs to detect explosive material in cars or trucks, special equipment for checking any persons and equipment entering official buildings, installation of portable ground to air rockets for shooting down kamikazi airplanes (striking against the White House) and establishment of an air command centre near the White House to check all air traffic around the building.

2) The establishment of special forces and shock troops for use against terrorists. For this purpose a special security detachment with 42 officers was set up around the country for use in case of emergency. Similar detachments were formed in the Army. In the State Department a counter terrorist group was established which could also be used for emergency planning of counter terrorist operations. Let's pause for a while and study the case of an Institution which certainly will attract our special interest. It is called Critical Enterprises Centre and works as a branch of the counter-intelligence service. It has three rooms without windows on the 6th floor of the counterintelligence service in Pennsylvania Street. The center has safeguarded telecommunication with all the counterintelligence offices around the country. T.V. screens in connection with cameras are able to scan every sensitive target of terrorists in the United States. It is also equipped with terminals for communication with the computer centre of the counterintelligence service and in some areas with the CIA and the information service of the Army. It also communicates with all the detachments and the police patrols. Aerial views show the most important airports and the nearby buildings, and maps with light indicators show the most sensitive targets. The Centre also maintains a direct tele-communication with the White House, Pentagon and Intelligence Services around the USA and abroad. The Head of the Centre is Oliver Reaval, deputy of the Counterintelligence Service, responsible for the detection of common crimes. The Centre also maintains telecommunications with the Counterintelligence Data Bank. It also has an electronic device which is used for enterprises like 'Operation salvation'. This device works with laser diskettes, computer unit and photo techniques producing three dimensional pictures of the interior and exterior of a 'sensitive' building. Similar pictures can also be taken of all the major Institutions, the counterintelligence buildings, banks etc. The purpose is to develop data banks with information

on the most likely targets for terrorist attacks. That 3-dimensional picture gives a complete view not only of the exterior but of interior areas as well. It gives the impression of pictures taken with a portable video-camera.

There have also been established some Institutions and Brain Banks with specialised teams for research into the problem of terrorism and particularly its practical aspects. Some of the best known centres are the following:

1. RAD Company. Scientists like Brian Jenkins and Bruce Hoffman are occupied with problems of right wing terrorism in Europe, and also Michael Randu who studies terrorism in Latin America.

2. Strategic and International Studies Centre in Georgetown where Robert Cooperman and the former Chief of CIA, Colby, are working. They are employed with research into International Terrorism and suggest relevant measures inside the country and abroad.

3. International Problems Centre in Harvard University. The most prominent representative is A. Offrie who is studying matters of information and counterintelligence related to terrorism.

4. The Heritage Legacy – the basic brain centre of planning against terrorism. It advises semi-military operations in Cambodia, Laos, Vietnam, Angola, Ethiopia, Afganistan, Nicaragua, Iran and Libya. The institute recommends that Syria, Libya, Iran and North Korea are declared 'terrorist countries'. Main representatives of this institution are Brucelec, Wyneront, Richard Schultz and the President's Advisor in national security matters, Richard Allen.

The most important terrorist groups which are the subject of intensive research by CIA are: 'Muslim Brotherhood', the extremist group of 'Al Daua', the 'Libertarian Islamic Middle Eastern Group', the muslim organisation 'Hizb Allah' all fighting against American military targets and others.

It is remarkable that in a country like the USA the terms 'terrorism' or 'terrorist activity' are neither elaborated legally nor confirmed in any legislature. The counterintelligence service uses its own terminology for the definition of any kind of violence as either terrorist action or common crime, but it has never published the criteria or the evidence which define a terrorist action. This allows the distortion of evidence towards terrorism and the deception of common sense to the benefit of the government.

USA government and NATO's members are spreading the dogmatic concept that the main sources of terrorism are the revolutionary and national liberation movements around the world. The USSR, Bulgaria and other socialist countries, have been accused of terrorist activities when supporting these movements against imperialism. The recent intensity of terrorist attacks against American delegations outside the USA gave a chance to Reagan's Administration to stir up a propaganda campaign. The volume of this campaign was greater than the danger of terrorist incidents against USA really warranted. The purpose was to give an excuse for an aggressive foreign policy, and also to increase spending on the war against international terrorism. The socialist and undeveloped countries proved to be an easy source of terrorism; And, of course the USA had to convince public opinion inside the country and abroad that 'preventive operations of punishment' and also the use of military force against national liberation movements or independent countries was warranted as a specific against terrorism.

Socialist International foreseeing all these factors and reporting them from time to time to the public, has earned the intensive hostility of the USA against the brotherhood of Socialist and Socialdemocratic Parties. This hostility has become more obvious since the resurrection of Socialist International and because of its present vitality which has been a result of Willy Brandt's presidency.,

Before Olaf Palme's assassination and in relatively recent times, the political observers studying the intensive hostility of the last 30 years have come to the conclusion that the main reasons are:
– the zig-zag movement of USA Administration towards external problems, the unpredictable policies of Washington, the advantageous decisions and the indifference of the NATO members for the political views, have been proven the main characteristics of the tactic of American sovereignty.

The closed shop policy of the USA has created a series of divisions in the Western World to the benefit of other political forces. Socialist International is one of those forces and its leaders are now convinced that Washington's policy is not the proper one to serve the western interests and save the reputation of the west.

– That's why American's do not like the 'resurrection' of Socialist International. The American Government are concerned about Socialist International views on the subject of nuclear armament and the competition of East and West. Socialist International supports the peace movements and proposes cooperation with the USSR, it also favours Santinistas' Revolution in Nicaragua and supports the liberation movements in the third world countries. As socialist International becomes more organised, Americans see the ghost of 'cryptocommunism': the fact that socialists accuse Washington of forcing a repetition of Chile's history in Nicaragua and Salvador, of racism and interference in South Africa and Chad, is feeding the imperialist propaganda.

– Americans were especially aggressive towards Willy Brandt, Olaf Palme, Walter Hacker, Calevi Sorsa and Byrd Carlson, but they are getting less so in their criticism of Socialdemocrats in South Europe. The United States are always wary of every kind and colour of socialism and socialdemocrats because criticism against the system is inherent in socialist theory. But lately American opinion has been dividing the socialist trend into two categories: good and bad. Good socialists are those who are in opposition, without any power, who pose no threat to take over the government. In this group are also included those who 'forget' their political slogans when they attain power and accept the American presence in Europe. For example, the saying 'A good socialist is a dead Socialist' does not apply to Francois Mitterrand – for Mitterrand is in every way acceptable, as in order to save the French franc from destabilization he made important concessions to Washington.

Felippe Gonzales, the exceptional 'Southern' socialist, has maintained his relations with USA on a friendly level, because of American capital which has been invested in Spain. Portugal accepted Spain into NATO because of U.S. threats to freeze their credits. With a few words, Americans control the 'southern' socialists perfectly. Italians and Portuguese support Reagan's 'zero solution' and also enrich their propoganda slogans with anti-Soviet ones.

France not only gives their moral support to the installation of Pershing and Tomahawk missiles, but they also support propaganda that the Soviet Union excels in military might and thus threatens the balance of power in the world.

The position of the conservative wing of Socialist International towards the Third World silently favours Washington's plans:

Mitterrand supported the punishment of Argentina but did not say a word against Israel.

France not only gave moral support to the installation of Pershing and Tomahawk missiles, but they also support propaganda that the Soviet Union excels in military might and thus threatens the balance of power in the world.

Socialist Party) from its original anti-imperialist course. For the time being, Andreas Papandreou (PASOK's leader) is considered a 'bad' socialist because he is resistant to pressures not only from the USA but from Socialists who are flirting with Washington.

As much as the American government suffers from an allergy against the Socialist wave, it is still able to find antidotes everywhere. It has already found some faithful friends who can be bought with money, amongst the vexatious host of S.I.'s members. With these friends they exchange compliments, investments and missiles.

'A Red Rose for Olaf Palme'.

16

3
A Different Opinion Regarding Socialist International

I usually give, as much as is possible, a chance for the reader to form an all round view of the subjects under discussion. Here is a study by Spyros Dendrinos, which was published in the monthly issue of the 'North-South' magazine in the January-February issue of 1986 which due to the specialist nature of the magazine failed to achieve sufficient circulation.

Does Pasok take the Leadership of Socialist International?

Socialist International: Is that a big 'brotherhood' of the socialists around the world? Or an Utopia? Or an illusion? It has been accused of various interventions into the socialist parties especially of the south, and also into the national-liberation movements of the Third World. Its members are all the socialist and socialdemocratic parties of Europe – except PASOK of Greece up to the present time – but also Bulent Etzevit's party of our known 'Attila'. In their conventions every 2–3 years they are seeking a formula to achieve the most effective intervention, as a united international organisation, into the areas of the world, where, it is obvious, human rights or peace are in danger. Socialist International can also intervene as a negotiating power in times of crisis, as an advisor in that situation.

Under the auspices of Willy Brandt, the President of S.I., the famous conclusion of Brandt's Committee for the situation in the Third World was written, and was accepted by everybody. The reputation and power of W. Brandt as former Chancellor of W. Germany has put him among the highest of the western political figures, with the most important aim of solving promotion peace talks and solving disputes between North and South. In order to understand better the abilities of S.I., let's examine an example: A few years ago in the revolutionary Iran of Ayatollah Homeini, as the world knows, the problem of American hostages occurred. A team of three European leaders undertook to visit Iran.

Socialist International in Iran of Homeini.

It is true of course that the three European socialist leaders who undertook the mission to Teheran were not exactly a delegation of S.I., and their direct purpose was not to free the American hostages. Their intention was to make a report for S.I. and they claimed that the subject of the hostages was merely brought up during the discussions with the Iranians and nothing else.

The relative indefinition and obscuring of issues is no accident. That's the way that S.I. operates. They are usually teams formed from the party leaders, (either in power or not) and meet with national parties, whose political aspects and programs cover a wide range, despite the common acceptance that 'socialism' is their main target.

The team destined for Teheran consisted of the following members: Bruno Kreisky, Prime Minister of Austria, Olaf Palme, ex Prime Minister of Sweden and Felippe Gonzales of Spain. These three met with all the members of the Revolutionary council of Iran – something that no other western politician had ever succeeded in doing – and other left wing democrats who had been very important in opposition to the Shah but, after the revolution lost their power. The only exclusion was Ayatollah Homeini himself, who did not meet the three delegates.

Olaf Palme, when he returned to Stockholm, reported during a telephone conference that he found Iran's political movements seriously dedicated toward the matter of national independence. He also added that among the political factors he had encountered, he found some facts which he could not understand because they looked uncertain.

The main purpose of this mission was to 'bridge the gap'. According to Gonzales', the spokesman, the three socialist leaders believe that S.I. can play a very constructive role in Teheran because 'S.I. had no ties with the Shah and his regime, while on the other hand it is actively involved in the Third World'.

This is a relatively recent success. In 1976 when a convention took place in Geneva and Willy Brandt was elected as president, S.I. decided to accept parties of countries other than Europe. Now under the umbrella of Socialist International there are 39 countries with 80 million votes.

Prehistory of Socialist International

The term 'International' was employed in 1864 with the first conference organised by Karl Marx in London. The second attempt, about 1876, was unsuccessful, so it was postponed until 1889 in Paris. It went through many factions and disputes during the First World War and the Russian Revolution. Finally Lenin established the Third International. During World War II Stalin dispersed it for diplomatic reasons. He tried to renew the statute of International establishing COMINFORM. Nikita Khrushchev and Leonid Breznieff though, found less typical ways to impose

Moscow's leadership upon as many communist countries as possible. The more or less marxist but not communist parties which did not want to be part of the Third International of Lenin, have stayed with the Second International.

In 1951 the present day Socialist International was founded in Frankfurt. Its programme, that is the establishment of social justice inside and between countries, and the end of every form of oppression is general enough, so it can include marxist political views or non marxist ones (like social-democrat).

A few years ago, one of the most important of S.I. problems did occur: This problem was, if, and how much, could Democratic Socialists work together with the communists. Because of their internal problems, W. Germany with H. Schmidt, Spain with Felippe Gonzales and Portugal with Mario Soares were against every kind of cooperation. On the other hand, Francois Mitterrand of France and Bettino Craxi of Italy supported cooperation with communists. German social democrats supported Soares when he was facing the communists in the elections in Portugal.

The new focal point, which is the relations between North and South (not East and West) faced the team of member countries of S.I. with new temptations. The old term which separated the 'Democrats' from the other socialists was based on their acceptance of the multi-party system. It is however hard for this criterion to be applied to the Third World. Any party member of S.I. is entitled to request and receive help from his comrades. This entitlement worked in favour of the National Revolutionary Movement of El Salvador which was accepted when it united to take power from the military oligarchy. Now they are opposing, with all the left wingers, the centre party which is supported by the USA.

An International Committee has been established which is occupied in drawing up a foundation plan to be submitted to the Convention of 86. This new plan will leave the term 'Social Democracy' as flexible as it can be. In this way it is hoped that countries with no present qualifications will decide to participate also. By these means once again in S.I.'s long life, the brotherhood is trying to identify with the modern spirit and in spite of European opinion that the real threat to peace is the unequal distribution of wealth among the countries of the world, the differences between East and West will eventually surface and become the first priority. The effort to widen the borders of S.I., especially in Latin America, Africa and somehow in the Arabic World, reflect European Socialists belief that the relations between North and South will be the basic problem in the future.

Brandt's Proposal to Andreas Parandreou

Socialist International has made a lot of efforts to include PASOK in its members. We have been informed that Willy Brandt, as a last effort, recently sent a delegation to Athens to propose to the President of PASOK, Mr. A. Papandreou, that he undertake the leadership of Socialist International in 1986. This comes as an award for Papandreou's efforts to promote peace and disarmament, and also for being the chief author of the famous Declaration of the Six Leaders for Peace and Disarmament. Of course PASOK participates as an ordinary observer at S.I.'s conventions at one time or another in various places in the world. A few years ago, also under the guidance of Papandreou, PASOK tried to build the foundation of a new form of International, the Mediterranean Socialist International. They appeared to make remarkable progress for a long period of time but there were obstacles in their way, such as: the sudden tensions caused by the Middle East crisis, the differences inside the Arab World, the continuous and destructive war of expansionist Israel against Lebanon and the Palestinians etc., and the unwillingness of some European leaders, like Gonzales and Mitterrand to continue with this Mediterranian effort. The movement, was therefore, although it had developed a lot of activity with Mediterranean conventions in Athens, Bremen, Malta, Barcelona and Algiers, forced, due to circumstances, to adjourn for the time being.

One outcome was the creation of an office, the Mediterranean Socialist Parties and Liberation Movements Administration (P.S.O.M.) which is however in a rather inactive state.

The Chief Workers of P.S.O.M.

For the record we refer to the most important associates of Andreas Papandreou in that great effort, the flame of which is not yet completely quenched: Carlos Papoulias, now the Minister of Foreign Affairs, Manos Kafetzopoulos, representative of PASOK at that time and now Ambassador to Libya, Pericles Nearchou, Advisor of the Prime Minister, Vassilis Constantineas, now Secretary of International Relations of PASOK, Iannis Matzouranis, advisor of the Prime Minister, Manolis Poniridis, Ambassador to Sweden, and Theodoros Stathis, member of Parliament. In today's political circumstances, when international organisations, interventions and roles are re-examined and re-considered in the light of Geneva's constructive meeting between Reagan-Gorbachev, the resurrection of S.I. is not an impossible dream, in spite of the huge differences between its members.

And Two Footnotes

1. In connection with the above regarding the initiative of the Six and the unanimous Declaration made by them, we have to add the following for the record. The last international initiative was a proposal by Andreas Papandreou, Prime Minister of Greece and leader of PASOK, Olaf Palme, Prime Minister of India, De La Madrid, President of Mexico, Alfonsin of Argentina and Nierere of Tanzania, in support of disarmament. The proposal was adopted by Pope, the Secretary of the United Nations, also by governments, political parties and peace movements.

The proposal was announced on 23 May by A. Papandreou and O. Palme on the American T.V. Channel ABC, the conference broadcasting live in the USA and by video recording in many European countries.

All the statements referred to a mission for peace as well as to the dangers of nuclear disaster in the event of the dialogue for nuclear disarmament failing, and are of exceptional interest. We give below the relevant paragraphs of the Declaration of the Six Leaders:

'We confirm our belief in tolerance and mutual understanding to include wide international cooperation and respect for the rights of every country to have a peaceful, safe and independent existence; also in the people's right to organise their lifes according to their own beliefs. It can not be secure if only one sided. That's why we give a terrible importance to the freeze of nuclear competition, which will allow for the renewal of the talks on nuclear disarmament to take place.

The common security and the avoidance of a nuclear war which threatens to eliminate the entire human race is an inalienable right of all nations. People all around the world demonstrate as never before their fears for the future. This open movement towards peace and disarmament and the encouragement of a well informed public will significantly encourage governmental attitudes towards the freezing of the nuclear weapon race.

We believe in human ability to overcome the differences existing today and to create a world free from the shadow of a nuclear war. The power and intelligence of the human race must be used, not for the development of weapons of disaster but for the exploitation of all sources of wealth on our planet in such a way that all people can enjoy a safe life in a global system free of wars and based on peace and justice.

Today the world depends on the balance between war and peace. We hope that our combined efforts will bring about a good and a positive result'. That was the Declaration of the Six.

2. Socialist International accepts PASOK as a simple observer with no

right of speech or vote, as it has done with a number of other national-liberation movements of the Third World. At the same time however it exercises some pressure on the leaders of certain political parties who play important roles in the international political scene.

Socialist International at the Present Time

The subject of this book, regardless of the general value and significance of its contents, is very opportune most especially for Greece. In the critical, dangerous and troubled times in which we live, (threatened by the arms race and competition between the two superpowers) the subject of S.I. is on the top of the agenda, for this international organisation fights against armament and against nuclear weapons; that is why S.I. incurs the furious hostility of the USA as evinced by CIA. Socialist International becomes a subject most appropriate to Greece because of the following: 1) The Greek Prime Minister completely adopts the political views of S.I. on disarmament and the initiatives of the Six. 2) PASOK now is negotiating to join S.I. officially as a member and some proposals have been made to undertake the presidency of Socialist International.

Therefore, everything written about S.I. and most particularly this present book, which is the first circulated in Greece on this subject, is of great relevance and of interest for its topicality. The author's purpose is to inform, as best he can, all Greek readers on the subject of S.I. and to give a wide view in that respect, explaining the reasons why S.I. has become a target for the CIA.

If the reader finds deficiencies, which certainly do exist, let him take note of the absence of any previous similar books on this subject and please believe that even apparently simple books require a lot of effort and time for the collection of material and the process of publication.

4

The Last Convention of Socialist International in Lima? Peru was 'Awash with Blood'

The 17th Convention of Socialist International was the first ever organised in Latin America, but the known reactive forces of the USA in cooperation with the local associates of CIA covered with blood the whole scene of the Convention in Lima, Peru.

The Convention came to an unsuccessful end suddenly on Sunday 22 June '86 (something which had been expected since 20th of June following the massive killings of prisoners in Lima). At the end of the Convention, which had been planned for Monday the 23rd of June, S.I. in its official final summing up, pointed out among other things the following: '... we express our serious concern about possible atrocities during the reprisals which will follow the riot in Lima's prisons, where about 300 people were killed by the Peruvian army...'

The re-elected President of Socialist International, W. Brandt, in his last press conference, also said; '...The President of Peru, Allan Garcia, has promised the organisation to form a congress committee which will investigate the case. Participating in this committee will be members of the opposition parties and independent political figures...'

In the Declaration of S.I. it was stated that the President of Peru, Allan Garcia, recognised the seriousness of the situation and guaranteed that he would not be himself involved in the investigation inquiring into the violation of human rights, also that 'the doors of Peru will be open to International Organisations to be convinced accordingly'. Allan Garcia's committments were the outcome of much hard negotiations between himself and representatives of S.I., because Spain and Venezuela were asking for public condemnation of the Peruvian government for the atrocious massacre of unarmed prisoners, who were killed in cold blood and who, as members of the local party 'Centro Luminoso', were in prison for their political beliefs.

It is also of note that the Peruvian organisation 'Andrean Legal Committee' stated that in the bloody incidents in Lima's prison the military authorities made no attempt at negotiation but went ahead and committed the massacre in cold blood. The same Committee pointed out that the military authorities also refused the examiner's request to visit the prisons immediately in order to apply the regulations of the Charter of Human Rights. The military authorities also would not allow the examiners to participate either in the identification of the deaths nor in the autopsies, which were secretly performed.

The General Secretary of the governing party, American People's Revolutionary Union (APRA), Mr. Armando Vallianuevo, who had represented his party at the convention of S.I., explained that the prisoners' corpses were buried 'for medical reasons' but he denied that they had not given any notice to the families of the dead men. The unacceptable and atrocious event in Lima's prisons overshadowed the convention of S.I. as could be expected. From the works of the convention many important results had been anticipated on basic problems of Latin America. That's why many of the representatives on leaving Lima expressed the opinion that, possibly, an extraordinary meeting had to be convened soon.

It must be mentioned though, that some socialist leaders of high standing like F. Gonzales of Spain, B. Craxi of Italy and G.H. Brynland of Norway did not come to the commencement of the conventions, thus leading some people to believe that the convention was about to be sabotaged and that there had been some suspicions of this all along.

Other terrorist actions also affected the works of the convention. First, the Centero Luminoso welcomed the represenatives with three bombs in the hotel where they stayed, while the revolutionary movement 'Tupac Amaru', a partisan group active in the cities, occupied the offices of four press agencies in Lima on 23rd of June.

We must also add that even as 400 socialist leaders of 75 political parties from all over the world left Lima on Sunday evening a horrible TV program about the prison's monstrosities was being transmitted, a program which was interrupted after a while because of 'technical problems'.

The mere fact that the 17th Convention of S.I. took place in Lima, Peru, indicates the direction of the movement since the election of W. Brandt as President in 1976, that is to pay more attention to the problems of the Third World countries, especially of Latin America.

We must remember that S.I. has substantially contributed to the development of European solidarity against the military Juntas of Argentina, Brazil, Huruguay, Bolivia and Chile and has proven to be a positive factor for Democracy, which has overcome in all these countries except Chile.

If one considers that all these military Juntas had been given money by the USA and also takes into consideration the work of the CIA in these and other countries, then one may easily understand why S.I. has become a permanent target of the CIA and realise why CIA ruined the last convention of S.I. with those bloody riots in Lima's prisons.

It is not accidental also that the previous convention of S.I. in Portugal in 1983 was marred by bloodshed, remembering that inside the convention's buildings, a Palestinian leader, named Sartui, fighting for a peaceful solution of the Middle Eastern crisis, was killed.

In both these conventions, in Portugal and Peru, S.I. was planning to discuss in a quiet manner, and to take reformative decisions on, problems of the Third World countries. CIA though, the 'big mama' of international terrorism knows how to disrupt proceedings at a crucial moment. Thus, applying their methods in Lima, they succeeded in interrupting the convention of S.I., causing it to close one day earlier in a state of complete confusion as a result of the death of 300 defenceless prisoners. This incident even forced the President of Peru, Mr Allan Garcia himself, to call the tragic event a massacre in cold blood, committed by the military of his country.

In spite of what happened in Lima, the decisions which had already been taken and announced in the manifest of Socialist International in Lima, also the statements made by the President W. Brandt in his speech, contain, without doubt, interesting views and indicate generally the desire of the progressive powers of European and other countries to find a solution to the problems of the oppressed nations of the world; oppressed mainly by the USA.

S.I. assists with all its power the countries of the Third World, especially those of Central America. It supports the plans of the 'Contadora' team, while at the same time criticising the lack of political pluralism in Nicaragua; it emphatically condemns the expansionism of Reagan's administration which gives money, through the CIA, to the Contras.

As far as disarmament matters are concerned, S.I. is on the side of stopping nuclear and chemical weapons tests, respecting the SALT-2 agreement and the creation of nuclear-free zones. The views of S.I., towards Cyprus, Afganistan and many other international problems are unequivocable and have lately helped S.I. to widen its horizons and to establish its reputation.

It is characteristic that in Latin America for example, a series of movements which are not totally socialist ones, such as APRA in Peru, Argentinian Radicalism, National Front for the liberation of Salvador Farabunto Marti and Santinistas, have official contact with S.I.

However, the power of S.I. to influence West European governments has been reduced because on the one hand socialists are not in the Governments of important countries like W. Germany and France, and on the other hand, whenever socialists are in power they tend to forget the policies of S.I. in favour of their own particular interests. It is characteristic that in the convention of 1983 the French socialists, though in power at that time, did not support the decisions for disarmament, but supported the opposition parties. Something similar has occurred with the problem of the debt of the 3rd World. The West European governments, including the socialist ones, excepting only Switzerland, have been aligned with the USA, giving a special importance to the relations betweeen the indebted countries and the credit banks and refusing to acknowledge that the debt is mainly a political problem, the solution of which will be of benefit to the international community. It is also important that S.I. considers that the Santinistas government in Nicaragua has not yet fulfilled its committments to restore a policy of 'non engagement' of political pluralism and mixed economy. In the last resolution of the 17th convention of S.I. in connection with the problem of Latin American and the Carribean, it was pointed out that: According to our judgement the process of legislation, development and attainment of these targets has not yet been realised. The convention approved the report of the Special Committee for Central America, which, headed by the socialdemocrat Carlos A. Perez of Venezuela, visited all the countries of Central America and USA. The committee asserted that 'Nicaraguan dialogue between the government and opposition parties (even Church) had not made any progress in spite of the fact that it is a necessary step in order to ensure the wide spread and peaceful evolution of democracy in this country'. The resolution of S.I. for Latin America also condemns Reagans's administrational policy of economic boycott and the grant of military support to the Contras who fight against the independence and the sovereignty of Nicaragua.

Socialist International also expresses 'their constant sympathy and support' for the initiative of the Contadora group, and points out that it is essential to stop any assistance from outside to groups which act illegally to aid rebels, in addition to stopping all international military exercises, freezing the armament supplies, eliminating the presence of foreign military advisors and making an agreement of non-aggression among the five countries of Central America. This is the way to obtain national reconciliation and the recognition of human rights; also people's freedom will be respected in the development of a good peripheral and international cooperation.

With regard to the Salvador crisis, the following are marked in the last resolution of S.I.: 'The US government must not try to label this conflict as yet another East-West competition, but it must seek for a solution within the special situations and standards of Latin America'. In the same text, S.I. also expresses solidarity towards the people who are fighting against dictatorships in Chile and Paraguay and generally takes the side of right in many other problems which occupy the modern world.

Because the main subject of this book is S.I., and since the opening speech of its president W. Brandt and the Manifest of the 17th Convention of S.I. in Lima have never been published in Greece until now, we quote both of them.

5
Willy Brandt's curriculum vitae

Willy Brandt was born on 18 December 1913 in Lubeck, illegitimate child of Martha Fram who died in 1969. His real name was Herbert Ernst Carl Fram. He finished the High School in Lubeck in 1932. As a high school student he joined the socialist youth movement 'Socialist Labour Youth' and he wrote for 'People's Messenger of Lubeck' the newspaper of the German Socialdemocratic Party. Under the protection of Julius Leber (an antifascist who was murdered by the nazis) Brandt became a member of the German Social democrat Party at sixteen. In 1931 he joined a left splinter group of the party, because he thought that the Socialdemocrat party had compromised with the Nazis in an unjustifiable way. When the Nazis took over power he went underground with the pseudonym Willy Brandt. In April 1933 he left Germany in a small motor boat and went to Copenhagen where he stayed for a short period of time until he left for Oslo. There he studied History, while continuing his political activity. In 1938 German citizenship was denied to him, so he became a Norwegian citizen.

In 1936, as a Norwegian student in Berlin, he was the leader of the outlaw antifascist organisation METRO. In 1937 he went to Spain as a correspondent of the Republican party. Travelling through Holland, Belgium, France, England and Czechoslovakia he kept contact with socialdemocrat groups of German immigrants. During the surrender of Norway, on 1 May 1940, Brandt succeeded in avoiding captivity as a Norwegian soldier and went to Sweden. In Sweden he continued his career as a reporter from 1940 until 1945 in conjunction with his political activity, working in the International together with Bruno Kreisky. Since then, both men have maintained a very close friendship. From 1945 to 1947 he was a correspondent of the Scandinavian newspaper for Germany and for a limited period of time he worked as a Press attache in the Norwegian mission in Berlin.

Since 1947 he has lived in Germany, adopting the pseudonym Brandt as his last name. Nominated by Kurt Summaher' Brandt was elected in 1948 as representative of the administration of the German Socialdemocrat Party in Berlin. From 1950 to 1953 Brandt was a member, from 1954 Vice President, and from 1958 to 1962 President of the provincial office of the party in

Berlin. After Dr. Otto Zurr's death, Brandt was elected, on 3 October 1957, as Mayor of West Berlin, and he stayed in that position until 1966.

This period of time, when Brandt was Mayor of West Berlin, (included the Soviet blockade of this part of the city and Berlin's crisis in 1958 and 1961) has been of critical importance in forming his political anti-communist views. Brandt has no excuses for Grotteval breaking off from the German Socialdemocrat Party, something which, according to Brandt, had active support and pressure from the soviet occupation authorities.

International exposure of West Berlin's problems gave a chance for the talented politician and speaker, Willy Brandt to obtain world wide fame.

It has been said that Brandt's and E. Barr's political experience helped them to elaborate the foreign policy of the Socialdemocrat Party, which is known as a policy of small steps, explained with the concept of 'change through negotiation' (1963).

Together with E. Eichler and Herbert Wenner, Brandt was a pioneer in the elaboration of political programs of the German Socialdemocrat Party in Band-Godesberg in 1959. In 1961 he was, for the first time, candidate to the Party for the position of Chancellor. On 16 February 1964 Brandt was elected as President of the German Socialdemocrat Party taking over from E. Olenhauer.

Brandt and Wener played the main role in the formation of the coalition government of 1, December 1966, in which Brandt was Vice Chancellor and Minister of Foreign Affairs. From this position Brandt gave great assistance to the agreement concerning the French army in West Germany, following the separation of the French from the military branch of NATO, and also for the participation of W. Germany in the agreement for non expansion of nuclear weapons and for the preparation of the way for England to join the EEC. On 3-9-1968 also during the General Conference of UNESCO in Paris, Brandt won wide international fame with his political stance by which he refused to resort to violence. In the period of the great coalition he helped substantially toward the restoration of diplomatic relations with Rumania (31-3-1967) and Yugoslavia (31-1-1968) as well as the exchange of trading relations with Hungary, Czechoslovakia, Poland and Bulgaria.

The re-election of Brandt as President of the German Socialdemocrat Party in Nuremberg Convention (March 1968), by giving him the overwhelming majority of votes (325 to 5), gave him enough courage to break the ties with the Christiandemocrat Parties and to open up the way to a Social-Liberal coalition.

Of course he was helped by the break from the Liberal Democrat Party. On 2-10-1969 Bundestag elected Brandt as Chancellor and Scheel as Vice

Chancellor and Minister of Foreign Affairs, with just 2 votes less. In his declaration on 28-10-1969 Brandt put the outline of an active east west policy. He recognises the existence of two German countries (a rejection of Hollstein dogma) but without considering one another as 'foreign' countries. The 'Pangerman' Ministry is converted to Ministry of Interior German Relations. In 1970, by his own initiative, Brandt met Willy Stoff, (in March in Erfurt and in May in Kassel). Brandt has undoubtedly contributed to agreements between Germany and the East, such as the Soviet Union, Poland, East Germany, Czechoslovakia, and the four part agreement for West Berlin on 3-9-1971.

These agreements, also the meeting of Brandt with Breznieff (16-9-1971), greatly helped the preparation for the final conference in Helsinki. With reference to this, it is also noteworthy that Brandt (as Minister of Foreign Affairs in the great coalition) gave much assistance to NATO in their decision to start certain negotiations in Reykiavik in 1968, for the reduction of military forces in Central Europe. This is the first concrete decision of NATO based on the spirit of its double strategy, which is explained in Armel's report of the same year. This great activity of Brandt on the problem of Eastern policy was to cost him the position of Chancellor, when on 28-4-1972 in Budenstag, after a proposal made by the Christiandemocrat Parties, he failed to receive the vote of confidence. The result of this vote was a draw (247: 247 votes. due to the treason of the representatives of the Independent Democrat Party), so they voted again in November 1972 in premature partiamentary elections. Before that time Brandt and Barr managed to sign the agreement for the basis of relations between West and East Germany. This way the elections were converted to a referendum upon the matters of policy towards the East. The results were good for the German Socialdemocrat Party, which received the majority seats in Budenstag; also, in April, the convention of the party re-elected Brandt to the position of President with 404 votes out of a total of 428. In the middle of May 1973 Breznieff visited W. Germany for the first time – that visit marked the high spot of Brandt's achievements in Eastern Policy.

In the beginning of June, Brandt visited Israel for the first time as Chancellor. This was also the first time that a W. German leader had supportd the rights of the Palestinians and the other countries surrounding Israel.

Brandt greatly helped to initiate dialogue between Arab countries and the EEC, and he gave shape to an independent EEC policy towards the Middle East.

The economics crisis, mainly due to the oil crisis, was of consequence to the internal policy views of the Socialdemocrat Party and was the cause of many discussions inside the Party – concerning its economic and social policy, with which Brandt, because of his work load as chancellor, found it difficult to cope. The relations between Brandt and Wener worsened. The Guilliaum case gave Wener the chance to defeat Brandt, who resigned on 7 May 1974 and sank into deep depression. However his many friends (from the centre to the left wing of the party) made him stay in the Presidency of the Party and he succeeded in quickly overcoming the crisis (which was also of a personal nature because of the moral aspects of the Guilliaum case), due to his successful emphasis on his impressive foreign, political activity.

In the convention of the Socialdemocrat Party in Manheim in 1975, Brandt was re-elected with a great majority (407 votes out of the 436 registered). This gave him the encouragement (with Wener's help) to beat the extreme left wing (consisting mainly of young socialists under the leadership of Beneter who was a follower of the theory for state capitalism 'Stamocap') as well as the right wing, united under the organisation 'Fritz Erler'. Meanwhile the right wing Socialdemocrat, Helmut Schmitt, became Chancellor, and this event, while strengthening the position of the right wing Socialdemocrats, caused many left wing Socialdemocrats to leave the party and at the same time weakened the image of the Party to young people. These phenomena which Brandt could not cope with when Schmitt was in power, played a critical role in the establishment of the social and political positions of the Greens.

About the end of November 1976 Brandt was re-elected as President of the Socialist International and helped strengthen its influence in Latin America and Africa.

In March 1977 Brandt declared that he was ready to become President of the, so called, International Committee for 'North-South' which was founded due to the initiative of McNamara, (at that time President of the World's Bank). In February 1980 Brandt presented the first report of the Committee and in October 1981 he organised in Mexico a high level meeting on the subject of assistance towards countries in need of development. In 1983 the committee, under Brandt's guidance emphasized the urgency of the report with the theme 'Help in world's crisis – a program of emergency'.

As President of S.I., Brandt struggled to achieve a political solution to the Middle East crisis. In 1979 he was elected as number one candidate of the German Socialdemocrat Party in the W. European Parliament, but he resigned in 1983, because of the intensive duties of the Party. After his meeting with Breznieff at the end of June, 1981, Brandt was engaged with the idea of the creation of a nuclear weapons free zone in Northern Europe and also with the refusal to alllow the installation of new American middle range nuclear missiles. As President of S.I., Brandt, in December 1981, made some realistic statements concerning military law in Poland. Although Brandt was denounced by right wing politicians, he was re-elected as President of S.I. in 1982. Since the beginning of 1981 Brandt had started to follow the political line of turning the Socialdemocrat Party towards left wing social factors. This factor, as much as the rejection of the decision of Budenstag which allowed the installation of new American missiles, permitted the fast stabilisation of the voters and of the Party itself. The re-election of Brandt with an absolute majority in the position of President of the Socialdemocrat Party was a triumph for his political policy, and created a possibility for cooperation between the party and the Greens in taking over power.

Since the autumn of 1983, Brandt has participated actively in the mobilization of the peace movement. Under Brandt's guidance the work for restoration of the Band-Godesberg program was reinforced. This does not mean, as Brandt himself points out, that there is a change in the principles of the program, but demonstrates the return to a marxist position and the renewal of the democrat socialist theory with adjustment to the demands of the crisis in economy, technology and the natural environment.

Brandt announced that he wants this renewal to become a reality by 1988 but only a few believed in this target. Brandt published a lot of work dedicated mostly to the theory and practice of W. German and international social democracy.

The most siginificant of his works are: 'Meetings and views – The years 1960–1975' published in 1976, and 'On the left and free – My route, 1930–1950', which was published in 1982.

Brandt speaks English, French, Norwegian and Swedish. He loves to read, especially books on history, he also enjoys fishing or walking with one or two friends. He likes anecdotes and jokes. His first marriage, from 1941 to 1944, was with the Norwegian, Charlotte Torkildsen. The second one, from 1948 to 1979 was also with a Norwegian, Root Hanzen, from whom he got divorced a few months after a heart attack. In December 1983, at the age of 70, he got married, for the third time, to Briggite Zeebaher, who was born in 1946.

6
The opening speech of the convention of Socialist International in Lima

Before I start, I wish to express my warmest thanks to the President of the Republic and to our friends of APRA, who contributed so much to this convention here in Lima. All of us are glad to be here and we deeply appreciate the warm hospitality. I would like also, to welcome all the representatives, some of whom have come from long distances in order to attend this convention. I also congratulate the many observers and guests from all around the world, who are here with us, at this convention of Socialist International. I am sure that I express the general opinion by saying: we are glad we are here and will avail ourselves of the opportunity to express our solidarity with the forces of progress and social democracy in Latin America. We have the chance to express the most sincere feelings of sympathy towards the people of Peru and the President, Allan Garcia.

We know very well the difficulties which you have to face, a lot of which are not due to the internal problems of the country. We assure you, though, that you have friends all around the world, who will not abandon you. We are on your side in the battle against social conflicts and misery, for social conquests and economic progress. The forces of evil are threatening us from many sides: They took the life of our beloved brother Olaf Palme. We must understand though that there are circumstances under which it is not sufficient just to talk even though you can help in this way. There is no doubt that constructive ideas and decisive actions are the only means available to overcome all these destructive forces.

These days the Social International Forum is once again in a position to serve our attention and unite our powers:
– The powers which intend to stop the insane armament competition, to establish peace on earth and to use these efforts towards fruitful goals.
– The powers which understand how many things depend upon the attention paid by people to all global problems, like the continuous destruction of the natural environment and the global economic problems which have run out of control.
– The powers, also, which intend to continue and to reinforce the battle for individual and ecumenical human rights, the battle with which our

movement had been involved since its establishment with ties which are unbreakable.

Democratic socialism without human rights looks like Christianity without Christ.

With great satisfaction I found out that at this convention more women are present than have been before on similar occasions. Today though, who would doubt, that human rights include equality between men and women, not only formally, but in reality? Without doubt this is part of the distance we have to travel from a patriarchal society to reach a real humanist society. In our organisation we should ensure the complete and equal participation of women at any level of political responsibility. From this point of view we should not only give importance to what is discussed and decided on in the women's organisation of S.I. but also analyze and continue beyond that.

This convention in Latin America is a very important event for the development of our international community. Our meeting in Peru means that S.I. comes to Aya de la Torre's country, that means to the roots of 'Indo-Americanism'. This is not something self-explanatory. Maybe of no significance. I remember very well what Aya de la Torres, ten years ago at the Caraca's conference had to say. He referred to Goethe, the great German poet, to the point where Mephistopheles says that theories are all very well but only life is in a position to show the whole picture. What else does that mean, except that all truth in life is correct. So we have to pay more attention to the roots of democratic socialism in Europe, and not only there but to all possible contacts, such as the forces of Latin America, including the Carribean. Also there are the possible contacts which may connect you with similar movements and peoples of the same mind in Africa, in the Middle East, in Asia and the Pacific Ocean.

In spite of the changes in its organisation, S.I. has a history running back 120 years; however we are just at the beginning of the works which the people before us considered to be their particular duty. As a movement of ideas and as a means to pursue the work, based on these principles, the period of evolution is still ahead of us, if humanity is to survive. The securing of this survival is the target at which we aim.

Although S.I. is neither a super power nor a super party, it joins together more than 60 parties, 24 of which are in power, while the rest of them play the role of strong opposition. In S.I. are united 12 friendly and similar organisations. We have good, fruitful contacts with a series of political organisations, especially of the 3rd world countries. Since 1864, one of the purposes of the, at that time, small European club, established in London with the name 'International Labour Organisation' was to strive for a better life for the labouring class. The struggle for peace (against colonization, the setting of the fire of war and the armament competition) gave life to the renewed International in 1889. The shape we have achieved nowadays for International is a society which has developed a great deal and became truly international due to the changes in the world. At the same time, on this basis, the aims remain the same. The aims are the well being of the workers (and those who are not allowed to work), their liberation from exploitation and underestimation. At the forefront of our attention there is still the right of nations to self-government, the right to fight against audacious imperialism which exploits people as pawns in a game of chess, where people are not masters of their fate but merely victims of foreign powers' involvement.

The tradition of International as a movement for the liberation of the people can prove to be an inspiration to us. The memories of a strong tradition and of our undoubted successes, can help us maintain our basic principles in a world which becomes more and more complicated.

I think that we could end up with an agreement over a renewed declaration of our principles, until our next convention, three years hence: 35 years have already passed since the time when the purposes and duties of democratic socialism were expressed in the Frankfurt declaration. The preparation for the change of that declaration makes good progress among small groups. My opinion is that now we need wider discussion. In order to give real significance to the program of S.I. we have to make this a subject of serious consideration by all the member-parties. The declaration of Lima, which has to be voted by this convention, constitutes an important step in the right direction.

I hope I may be allowed to refer to some points of our work in the party. The committee, of which I was the president, has recently finished the study of a program plan which has, as its purpose, the reformation and the continuation of our program which was first approved in 1959. This is the Godesburg program. We did not have any difficulties during the agreement of our basic directions. The main difficulties were encountered during the examination of a series of new problems which have arisen since 1960 and continue up to the present time, such as:
– The complete acceptance of equality between men and women and the future conditions of work in times of increased automation.
– The demands for a more modern technology so they will be in a position to define any dangers to the people, something that is especially important after the accident at Chernobyl.
– The need for a common policy and democratization of labour.
– Criteria for economic development of such a kind that will be acceptable in

relation to the ecological and social results.

– And also, combination of the terms of law with the terms of welfare and the merging of these two in what, in Germany, we call 'Kulturstaat', that means a society orientated towards culture.

On the subject of our international orientation we will not repeat our previous declarations. Now, when the survival of all humanity is in danger, the question of how peace will be achieved must be re-examined.

The need for fundamental reformation of the International Economy became obvious. The same thing applied to a whole group of international organisations. This at least has great scope for a series of moves towards a general cooperation, even for integration.

Unfortunately, recently, the multi-sided management has suffered from many troubles. Even the United Nations Organisation has serious financial problems. The General Secretary of U.N. asked me to assist in the correction of a widely held but erroneus perception connected with the role of the U.N. Organisation. It is weird, we could say insane, that financial problems have become an obstacle to the U.N. function at the very moment when this International Organisation plays an even more important role than ever before. The world should know in fact, that the U.N. budget is only the same amount which could balance the N. York Fire Department budget.

In the frame work of S.I. we have to put together the ideas of democratic socialists of developed countries as well as countries where development seems difficult due to various obstacles. A union like this would provide us with additional facts, which might explain why that called by some of us 'Internalisation of the international' is not only possible but also necessary. What motivation and prospects could exist?

Socialist International as a global power of peace and social progress, for the preservation and development of the natural and social basis of life, is the continuation of a tradition which maintains the fire instead of keeping the ashes. This could inspire, indeed, our future work.

Our course from the Geneva Convention in 1976 has brought us now to Lima. We faced many serious obstacles. I will refer to conventions in Vancouver, Madrid, our meetings in Dakkar, Tokyo, Arousa and Gaboron and also those places which have made Latin America a peak of great importance to our organisation; That is in Caracus in Mexico in 1976, Lisboa in 1978, S. Domingo in 1980, Rio de Janeiro in 1984.

When I mentioned that we are at the beginning of our work I had also in mind the fact that our international community as an organisation could be reconstructed proportionally with the new demands. As an idea, rather than as an organisation, social democracy and democratic socialism has always been to the fore of international relations. This fact, though should not prevent us from attempting some reformations. If we want to give some satisfactory response to the circumstances which we could meet, we need to take some measures towards coordination of action and strengthening of organisational structure. In my opinion, some proposals towards this direction are necessary.

I would like to express my thanks and gratitude to the honorary Presidents and Vice Presidents, to our General Secretary and his associates and also towards those who carry a corresponding position in the counselling committees and to the series of friendly organisations.

The necessity for programmed activities and politically organised measures also arises from the temptation of neo-conservatism, which we have faced for some time now; a phenomenon showing up in many countries. According to their leaders, their campaign is turned against the ideas of international Social Democracy and against the concept of a state which guarantees social security. We can oppose them only if we do not abandon the concept and the historical accomplishments of the State which guarantees social security and only if we do not get bogged down in the defence of past successes.

The great fraud of the campaign of neo-conservatives can be found in the way with which a host of people can be totally cheated through promises of something which only a minority can possibly enjoy. That is a serious weakness of their campaign. We have to put the record right

We, the Socialdemocrats and Democratic Socialists, are on the side of expansion of individual liberties, while some others prefer only to write about these liberties. We defend the right to a better life and the personal happiness of individuals. What else does history show? The history of the Labour Party, of Liberation Movements, of Democratic Socialism? The history though reminds us that social corruption and the degradation of the majority is a very high price to pay for the well being of an aristocratic minority. History has shown that the conscientious talents of numerous groups of people must be used if progress is to continue. History has shown that individual freedom remains only a dream, while just a minority of people enjoy its comforts and benefits. The free game of capitalism leads to a very unbalanced distribution of opportunity and can only act to the benefit of this minority.

In contrast to what neo-conservative philosophy attempts to suggest, the democratic social state is not an obstacle to the wheel of progress but provides the very wheel upon which progress can ride. In other words, we must create a situation which can be understood by the majority, when we declare that we want a future based on cooperation rather than on competition.

We do not expect anything from the competitive greediness which is the basic philosophy of government. Without solidarity peace does not exist, neither between countries and peoples nor inside the countries.

We have always been followers of the principle that peace inside and outside a country must be preserved through Freedom and Justice. None could doubt that in these last years the hopes of the world have increased. The opposite. For many years now we talk of disarmament. In the reality we became witnesses of an armament race on a much bigger scale. If this does not stop, there is very little hope for the future of humanity. The fate of this planet may depend on a new way of living together, which could be decided between the two nuclear superpowers, something which is not impossible.

Now though you think that nothing has stayed alive from the Spirit of Geneva. We must appeal to every country which has its own military strength. Everybody has to understand, now, how stupid it would be if they close their ears to what the other side has to say. This also means that all serious proposals should be treated with seriousness, should be analysed and judged even if they originate from Moscow.

We have to study all the appropriate suggestions for reduction of weapons. This, in my opinion, is more important than the development of perfect weapon systems.

Everybody understands the differences between Democratic Socialism and authoritative communism. Everybody though knows of the basic obligation to protect peace, which is of greater importance than the comparison of idealogies.

Before anything else, a new way of thinking is needed which will answer the demands of the nuclear era. The two superpowers, as much as the rest of us, have to accept the fact that there is no other alternative to achieve general security.

Last October, in the special convention of Vienna, we tried to formulate our position on matters of security and disarmament. At that convention, representatives of both the superpowers, the People's Republic of China, India, Yugoslavia, the independent countries movement and the U.N. were present. We have to strengthen our appeals in such a way to: –

– Stop nuclear trials. Also to make an agreement to ban nuclear tests by either side, something which is so obvious that it can be accepted readily. Great importance must also be given to the meetings between leaders of the five continents which will be organised for this summer.

– To start new and serious negotiations for the withdrawal of missiles of

38

both superpowers which have been installed without any immediate necessity. To start, also, negotiations for the reduction of military personnel and of nuclear and conventional weapons.

We do not need the elaboration of chemical warfare or systems of massive extermination. Rather than these we need bread for the poor. We do not need weapons for space.

I have already mentioned that the situation of the international economy still causes some serious misgivings. Some objective conditions have been improved to a certain level, but massive unemployment still troubles even the so-called North Solution while the debt crisis has not slowed up for the South. Also the danger of new trade wars still exist.

We are glad to learn that the democratisation of Latin America has made great progress. We were in a position to offer our modest support to this effort and we will not compromise in any way, while Chile and Paraguay still retain a dictatorship and Central America continues with military involvements which do not allow this area to find its own political direction.

We must recognise that the U.S. helped the promotion of democracy in a series of countries in Latin America and the overthrow of Marcos in Philippines. We should point out, however, that there is a connection between debts and democracy, between development and peace, in order to come to correspondent conclusions.

In recent years we should be aware of Central America's crisis. This was not our choice. Our partners in Central America, even some in Washington, have kept us informed of the position of this subject. I realise that the 3rd World view the so-called North-South in a totally different way than do the European observers. In spite of all this, I believe that you will agree with me, if I say that the theory of revenge has always been destructive. Of course, international law must be respected by all of us, being compulsory not only for small but also for big countries. It is not a law applicable only in some cases.

The world does not need interventions like that in Nicaragua, neither can it accept occupations like that of Afganistan. I think that we must support in every possible way the peace initiative commenced from this area of the world.

This is the Contadora proceeding and the team of South American countries which are supporting the same. The efforts spent towards that direction are deserving of encouragement and support from S.I. and also from other European parties.

In this situation I think that the zones of our activity for the next years are predefined and they find place in the order of the day of this convention. The zones of our activity are defined partially by old problems and also by new focuses of tension. So, repeatedly, even without some significant success, we have tried to help in the stopping of conflicts in th Middle East. Without being fed by illusions it must be clear that we are going to offer cooperation whenever this is needed.

This does not concern Africa at all. I believe that our friends from Africa who are here in Lima, will realise that in the last few years, S.I. has made great efforts, something natural to us, to support their rightful aims in any way. During our meetings in Arousa and Gaboron it was made clear that, primarily, we support the struggle against apartheid. In my opinion, the new report of the exceptional political figures of the Community for South Africa is of significant importance towards that direction.

In April I visited S. Africa and when I was leaving I felt sad. The picture I saw was even uglier than I had previously thought. What poses great danger in S. Africa – and this was proven during recent days – is more than a verbal reaction against the pre-revolutionary situation. In reality we endanger a large number of people who are threatened with elimination. We cannot be silent on this subject. We should prove our solidarity through our actions.

We have always been in the front line of the battle against terrorism and for the restoration of human rights around the world. Our position remains immovable, even during discussion of this matter with the conservatives. For us, the problem of Chile, Cambodia, Middle East and South Africa is very important, since it's about illegal invasion and violations in the name of the security of the state.

The struggle for human dignity and human rights, against hunger and misery, is a duty which must suggest immediate actions. Nothing is more important than the fate of people who are in danger and the problem of how they can be helped to survive in the best possible manner. That was the principle of Olaf Palme whom we greatly miss. He has repeatedly declared, in front of us and in front of others that 'aparthied can not be reformed, but what you can do is to eliminate it'. He had been worrying about the Middle East crisis and in the name of the U.N. he tried to find a solution to the war in the Persian Gulf.

– Two years ago, when we met in Denmark, Palme said that whoever had a clear heart could never leave post-revolutionary Nicaragua alone.

– The authorisations bearing his name resettled new laws in the moral and real battle against armaments.

– Palme put his last signature on a document of the initiative of the leaders of the five continents.

All these – to add to his significant participation in the achievements of his country – had been given the inspiration and support of the strong tradition of Scandinavian Socialdemocracy.

I can not find any other alternative. I do not see any other way to peace and development. There is no other alternative to human rights and solidarity, there is no other hope. Because we will not receive anything for nothing we should put even greater efforts into this purpose.

'A Red Rose for Olaf Palme'.

41

7
Lima's Manifest at the Convention of Socialist International June 20–30, 1986

1. This convention in Lima is dedicated to the struggle for peace, to international economic development and the protection of the natural environment. These aims require co-operation between nations, and not a narrow-minded selfishness and cynicism. The paradox of the present time is that although the nations of the Earth are more independent than ever before, there is not a unified, decisive confrontation of the above problems. The post war system is not satisfactory and it has to become adjusted to the modern situations.

2. In the years which are left of this decade many political, economical and social phenomana will appear, which will have significant effects on, and will greatly influence the world, because they are more entwined with economic relations and ties than ever before.

3. That's why we give such importance to this historical convention of Socialist International in Latin America which has reference to these matters in Lima's government. President Allan Garcia showed the way, which will not just help Peru to a better future, but show how to achieve a general solution to the economic crisis for the decade of 1980.

President Garcia and his party, the Peruvian APRA, have inherited the idea of a continental struggle against imperialism, and for the liberation of Latin America, which had been expressed for the first time as an ideal by victor Paul Haya de la Torres. These are very good indications of a new Socialist manifest, which pays attention mainly to the global prospects of Socialism from the end of the 20th century to the 21st.

4. The internationalisation of every human aspect is a characteristic of the big, modern reality. The military, economic, social and political reality requires a new formulation of the basic principles of Democratic Socialism. Theoretically the Socialist movement was always international. Modern circumstances, though, require us to be bound with Socialism in action, more than ever before.

5. We examine the natural relations between East-West as a dramatic example of the present dependency on each other's problems. The

experienced politicians of this decade have learned that even poor countries debts endanger the wealth of rich countries. The hunger and the low accession always indicated the existance of moral violence; now though there are signs of a general crisis as a result of the unnatural, economic unification of the world, which reaches beyond our political, social and national boundaries. A worldwide solution of the problem is the only hope.

6. This is absolutely true, because the understanding that the world is entering a new era of continuous progress, based on national and international inequality is just too terrible. One of the basic causes is the tough conditions which were imposed on the Third World in the decade of the 80's, which pose a danger to the rich countries of this planet on one side, and plague the poor on the other.

This brings danger to the producers, who will clash with the hungry consumers; to the creditors who will clash with the bankrupt debtors.

7. Many of the complicated problems of the natural environment and of progress today are caused, to a great degree, by the widely spread misery and the unequal distribution of raw materials between the different nations and areas.

8. Meanwhile, if a sudden change in life on this planet is not to occur, then the armament's competition must be halted because the new weapon systems will throw away any chance we have of control.

9. The ongoing conflicts in Central America, the Middle East, the South African Republic, the Far East and other areas – will bring not only death and disaster but they will provide the motives for even greater interventions and wars.

10. The economically advanced western countries, which still endeavour to face the chronic inconstancy dating from the end of the post war recovery period and the 70's, will need to go ahead in structural reformations, because the unequal and contradictory restoration between the three worlds is already reaching its end.

11. The economy of the Eastern block is still in deep crisis, because of the non democratic and extremely centralising programme, the beaurocracy and the lack of every initiative. Obviously the future will force these countries to make sweeping changes in their views and will make structural reformations a neccessity in order to satisfy their needs and to participate in a successful economic exchange between North and South. Inside a world where all things are dependent on each other, the economics of those countries cannot stay isolated from the rest of the planet, and neither should they prove to be so isolated.

12. We devote our selves to the struggle for the establishment of international cooperation in the multi-sided activity of the U.N., which represents all nations in its fundamental charter, which has as its goal the protection of human rights, the satisfaction of essential needs to man, the preservation of peace and the security of all. In the present efforts to ignore the U.N.'s role by the partial stopping of financial support or by disregarding the whole system, where by minority views can be imposed, new actions have to be taken so the U.N. can be changed to a basic centre of international co-operation. Similar measures must be taken to move away the existing system of the U.N. and to include new commitments for discussions within the framework of this international organisation, and also to make efforts to increase the scope of its activities.

13. We discuss here in Lima, within the framework of an analysis of the general crisis of the world's economy, a clear idea for the new meaning which had been given to our socialist principles; this is the moment when changes of great importance are being studied. We hope, of course, to convert the end of the 80's to a less turbulent decade than it was in the beginning. However even such 'general review' is enough to show why we believe not only in the fact that we now hold the solution to these problems, but believe that we can contribute to the development of Socialism through work as much as by scientific knowledge, in coping with the modern crisis.

14. We consider the present convention in Lima to be an international event. The majority of parties participating are from the Third World. We appeal to the North as well as the East and West.

We have analytical data which reveals that humanity is involved in a general trend left, and we, as Socialists, offer a general solution, a political direction, sufficient to unite men and women all around the world.

1. The General Crisis

15. The main subject of the I.S. for the World's Economy, can be found in Albufeira's manifesto and the 'International Challenge' and also in the two reports of Brandt's committee which shows there is a need for a general solution to the North – South crisis. The disastrous reality and the even more disastrous potential of the global crisis caused by debts can make our biggest fears come true.

16. The crisis arises from the failure of the monetary system of Britain in 1971–1973. The development of this crisis coincided with the end of the decisive leadership of the Americans to the Economy during the post-war period, and with terrible monetary depreciation. In the period between 1965–1970 the percentage of GNP of economies of OECD, with which is

provided help by the developed countries reduced from 0.49 to 0.39 percent, and the role of the private investors started to grow.

17. Later in 1974 the price of oil quadrupled. The bigger western banks were feeling proud (not without reason) that they had succeeded in putting billions into circulation through the oil revenue and this way gave the Third World countries with no oil the chance to survive, and enabled the most economically advanced countries to avoid the depression.

They were right and they proved, unwillingly, the truth of one of our most important theories, that the massive transfer of capital from the North to the South is a critical point in the general solution of the world's economic crisis. At the same time the debts crisis of the 80's was started.

18. As a proof of the correctness of our strategy for a bigger and bigger increase of the monetary quantity in circulation, for the benefit of North and South, we agree that the banks manipulations proved to be 'de facto' successful.

In the period 1973–1984 the average annual degree of development of Third World countries with no oil, was 5.1% (in comparison with 5.8% in the period 1967–1972). A huge step up in energy prices followed. Independently of this, the degree of development of industrial countries decreased from 4.4% in 1967–1972 to 2.8% in the period 1973–1981.

19. It is worthwhile to mention this. The North earned a great deal from this policy of financing the South, because the rise of the developing countries provided export markets for the rich and strong countries. Consequently our theory for a general solution of the problems doesn't consist merely of abstract thoughts. This happened during the 70's; the actions though were wrong and uncoordinated, and didn't lead to a balanced development.

20. The reason for that unfortunate position can be found in the fact that the finance came from private Banks, instead of official agencies. That means that when the crisis came, profit making institutions, in most of the cases, could not legally service the loans, as could official creditors. The solution of the debts problem of the 70's has developed into the loan crisis of the 80's mainly because the international capital flow between North and South had been changed in guarantee from the bigger private Banks.

21. Later on the crisis worsened because of the capital flow caused by existing U.S. inflation, which instead of helping the situation caused the most severe depression of those countries which they can remember during the last 50 years. The interest rates increased. The prices of oil became known so the money flow changed direction from South to North.

22. The price of merchandise started to decrease more for the exporters

45

of the Third World during the economic depression of 1974–1975 in the developed countries. Later, in 1979, we had new increases from OPEC and higher American interest rates followed which led to the increase in energy prices and also caused the biggest economic depression in the West after the 'Big Depression'. These facts combined caused a whole economic disaster for the Third World countries. Also because oil prices started to decrease, even the developing countries which had sufficient raw materials for their industries re-examined their expenses. Loans and investments became problematic. It is true that the North's provisions decreased simultaneously with the prices of merchandise.

23. In different areas of the world we had different reactions to these changes. Latin America was hurt very seriously – four of the seven debtors coming from this area of the world, with debts reaching the height of 300 billion dollars. The Philippines had debts totalling over 13 billions. South Korea owed over 31 billions, but the authoritative government which took over power became economically independent following a policy of low individual payments and salaries which enabled them to achieve the repayment of the loan. Other Asian countries took similar measures and managed to make a profit out of anti-democratic reprisals and the subjection of leading international companies.

24. These problems got worse later because of the famous capitalist agreement which was imposed by the International Monetary Fund, which demanded bigger austerity, reduction of consumer goods, depreciation with the purpose of securing imports and reduction of exports. At the time these reductions were made it was moment of deep trouble. As a result the huge mass of Third World and especially Latin America's countries should pay (by the decline of their standard of living) the loans of anti-democratic establishments whose number increased due to the anti-inflationary policy of western conservatives.

25. Although this crisis hit hardest the poor nations of the world, at the same time it also influenced, negatively, the rich, because the debts were to private banks, rather than to governments. The neglect of these banks would lead to a basic monetary policy between the developed countries, mainly U.S.

26. At the same time as the decrease in living standards in the developing countries, the corresponding strategy on exports meant that basic western countries lost their foreign markets and came up against a new escalation of competition. 'Federal Reserve Bank' in New York estimated that in the period of 1981–1983 U.S.A. lost 250,000 labour positions as a result of the 40% decrease in exports to Latin America.

27. The consequences were so obvious to the governments of developed countries, that they did everything in their power to keep the International Monetary System from going bankrupt. In 1982 the U.S.A. helped Mexico and other countries-debtors, but they didn't face the basic causes of the crisis.

28. Even before the dramatic decrease in prices in 1986 a new page in crisis history opened and it became clear that the monetary structure as it stood couldn't be saved, as usually happens, by trade. Thus for example, if followed strictly, the demands of the International Monetary Fund to liquidate the debts would impose on the developed countries a huge trade deficit against the Third World countries.

29. In the spirit of the purposes of International Law and Social Democracy we accept the so-called 'Big Challenge' and the program of activities, which has been approved by this convention.

30. Positively we oppose the idea that Democracy is a privilege only for countries with a developed Economy. Thus, as always the people from the valleys are against the rich and the strong of the North; the same happens today when the Socialist of the South consider these masses of people independently from their different historical and political situations. That's why we are specially happy regarding the achievements of Democracy in the Third World countries in the last three years.

We send our greetings to the countries – members of this organisation and our friends, who participate in these events in many countries of the world. We dedicate our powers to the re-distribution of the means of production, and of wealth, for economic democracy, well being and social justice in the North and the South. That's why we support the democratic countries and above all the countries which are following democratic paths and who respect human rights.

31. Having in mind some of the main problems of the Third World countries, we demand the maximum reduction of income and an honest fight for the fulfilment of the U.N. conventions program for the abolition of every form of racial or national discrimination. Each of these phenomena, we show can still be found in democratic countries.

32. We don't believe that human rights and democracy is a not understood luxury for the Third World while these countries are led economically by the world's and national aristocracy. We believe that the redistribution of income and wealth, the restoration of women's rights and the fight against racial and national prejudice will be supported by all progressive forces aiming to accelerate economic growth, and they will make every preparation needed so that the progress of technology will be used as a

means for the liberation of humanity, not as a new form of oppression.

33. That's why all of us, from the North to the South, who are gathered here in Lima, declare it our moral obligation that the common political interests of the Third World countries are the most important problems which unite us and that they must be emphasised in the principles which will guide us for the coming years.

2. The Natural Environment and Natural Resources

34. We are witnesses of ever increasing errosion of the natural environment and the exploitation of our limited natural resources. We are witnesses to the destruction of forests and the devastation of whole counries with a disastrous effect on our health, the plundering of seas and lakes and the contamination of our drinking water. We are witnesses of everything that effects the atmosphere and human genetics. Very often our attention is directed towards the effect which external factors can have upon our health and towards the danger from industrial growth.

35. Chernobil's accident proved the global dimensions of our problems; that disaster has no natural borders. That accident also demonstrated the great danger of nuclear energy. Although all the countries, members of S.I., are opposed to nuclear energy, now is the time to start thinking about energy production without nuclear energy, and all countries must undertake the obligation to inform, and to learn about, all new inventions, or indeed any damages caused by nuclear factories.

36. Although we face a lot of problems with the natural environment, we have the knowledge and the means to solve them.

37. The general provisions for the biosphere have great significance also for national and international security. Human activities could seriously violate the balance of the natural environment. That would endanger normal conditions of life on our planet and could create international conflicts. The dependence on the natural environment and the effect civilisation has on the potential for political and social destabilisation is so obvious that it can't be disregarded. Ahead of us lies the important task of finding a longterm plan of action for the protection of the natural environment and control of natural raw material for the demands of economic and social development and also for a quiet and peaceful life on earth.

38. In the name of international co-operation we have to consider seriously these important facts:
– The technological progress and the exploitation of natural raw materials must be harmonised with the demands of the world's system.

– The industrial countries should undertake greater responsibility for the technical equipment of the Third World countries, which must be of high performance and suited to the natural requirements of the country. This technology must be economical.

– To pay more attention to the question of the natural environment in the programs of aid provision.

– The prohibition of the export of products or energy which are hazardous to the natural environment or are unacceptable to the recipient country.

– To make accessible most raw materials and to prohibit the cutting of trees or the fast elimination of woods in the Third World and industrial countries.

– To make more efforts to reduce air pollution within the national boundaries.

– To prohibit with international laws every action which pollutes the water of the seas and lakes or contaminates drinking water.

– To pay more attention to the problems of the working environment, to health and well being, in the industrial and developing countries.

3. Control of the Insecurity of Modern Times

40. Peace and disarmament are very important matters for survival, and for progress and freedom. The arms race threatens the existence of the human race. It stops effective works for economic and social growth and it is poison to the relations between people.

41. As independent individuals and nations we are deprived of the rights of life and survival, of the right of completion of growth in peace, freedom and solidarity.

42. Nuclear war will destroy the whole planet and all humanity. Let us not misunderstand: A nuclear war would be a major crime against humanity.

43. The arms race is not limited just to nuclear weapons. More and more efforts are being made towards the creation of new and even more destructive conventional weapons. The armament competition has got out of control. It is not enough if we stop the wars. We must eliminate the whole escalation of the arms race. At this point there are no winners, there are only losers.

44. Governments must understand that their demands for security can not be limited only to innovation in the war industry and other forms of extermination. The quality of the applied political system has to be changed, not the quality of weapons.

45. The real security is the security which is created only by friendship, when we conform with the needs of people. We need a new policy of

cooperation, confidence and sincerity, which has, as a result, the reduction of tension.

46. We think that all countries, especially the important military powers, have political, moral and legal obligation to stop this madness. There is a disturbing confrontation between this obligation and the negotiations for disarmament between the different countries. S.I. condemn the failure of all interested governments to achieve an agreement related to the most important matter of modern times. All countries must prove that they are striving not only to prevent militarisation taking control in the armament race but that they are not postponing indefinately the final outcome which is to make effective agreements.

47. USSR and USA asserted their readiness to abolish their nuclear arsenals, starting with a reduction of 50%. S.I. applauds this readiness but wants actions instead of words. International intelligence will be affronted if it becomes obvious that the declarations of both sides are not true. That's why the restrictions which were imposed by SALT-1 and SALT-2 need to be followed strictly by both countries in order to reach an agreement for any significant reduction of the existing arsenals.

48. The interruption of and later, the definite prohibition of nuclear trials will show that the responsible countries consider seriously the control of armament. In fact, all nuclear trials have to be stopped. S.I. sends to the US government a heartfelt appeal to change its negative attitude towards a reasonable prohibition of nuclear trials. The negotiations concerning this agreement must start again immediately and this agreement has to be signed without delay and be applicable to all the powers which have nuclear weapons.

49. S.I. stresses the importance of all or part of these measures in the service of peace and the easing of tension. Any proposal regarding the limitation or reduction of weapons, or any kind of measures taken for the decrease of armament competition and tension has to be considered seriously, and a positive answer has to be given. Every unreasonable refusal to proposals for disarmament is disastrous to international understanding, peace and security.

50. The prevention of the production of counter-attack missiles and counter-satellite systems, on earth or in space, is also very important. The agreement between the Soviet Union and the USA, which was signed in 1972, condemned the production of antiballistic missiles and must be preserved and promoted. Space has to be used for peaceful purposes only.

51. Strategic nuclear disarmament will also unite countries which are against the installation of nuclear weapons. The movement for the non

expansion of nuclear weapons must be escalated and also the prevention of their installation in order to promote the creation of nuclear free zones.

52. S.I. refers with satisfaction to the Tlateloko agreement by which a nuclear free zone in Latin America was restored and to the agreement for a nuclear free zone in the south area of the Ocean, which was signed in 1985. S.I. calls on all countries to co-sign these agreements and bring pressure to bear on the nuclear powers to keep these agreements by adding their support.

53. S.I. approves the peace initiative of the six leaders of five continents. This initiative intends to prove that the belief in disarmament is not just held by the nuclear superpowers.

54. We have to make every possible effort to achieve definite reduction of chemical weapons and their research and development. The proposal to make an agreement elaborated by both the Socialdemocrat Party of W. Germany and SED of E. Germany can be acceptable as a two-part and peripheral plan of weapons reduction which goes beyond the borders of national alliances and is based on the theory of tension reduction and general security.

55. In view of the Geneva negotiations for the complete prohibition of chemical weapons, S.I. calls on the USA and all other powers to stop producing any kind of dual neuroparalytic gases. We condemn the use of similar weapons and all violations of the protocol of Geneva of 1925.

56. The USSR and the USA must stop immediately the further development of middle range weapons and come to an agreement for the two-part reduction and abolition of the existing weapon systems.

57. Disarmament control should not allow the free production of conventional weapons. The relation between those and nuclear weapons must be stressed and requires the taking of new decisive steps with regard to conventional armament. The Stockholm convention and the Vienna talks will produce positive results and lay the foundations for European disarmament.

58. Reduction of the arms trade must be included in any agenda on arms control. S.I. applauds the Peruvian initiative regarding the stopping of the provision of weapons in this area.

59. During the 40 year function of the U.N. it has proven to be the main and permanent arbitrator in international relations. The U.N. though was not supported in its basic mission. A great collaboration between all the countries is needed to unite their powers under the U.N.'s name and to stop the continuing peripheral conflicts and the creation of new focuses of tension.

60. S.I. condemns every expression of violence which is in opposition to the statutory Charter of the U.N. Socialist International is concerned by the increasing number of interventions as a means of resolving international, peripheral and national conflicts.

The world should not be pushed down the path of revenge. Terrorist activities have started to shake national and international life. Terrorism can not be examined as a different form of war or armed conflict. The threats of terrorism are turned against every aspect of normal life and strike mainly at the unprotected. Terrorism begats terrorism and consequently carries direct responsibility for the escalation of violence. Terrorism prevents rather than helps the solution of political problems. Democratic socialists take this chance of expressing their disagreement with this extreme method of action. They firmly declare that there is nothing that can excuse terrorist activities. That's why Democratic Socialists make an earnest appeal for the return of peaceful, poltical methods of non violence and the isolation and condemnation of those who continue to use terrorism as a means of achieving their political purposes.

61. The basic problems of our days, such as hunger, unemployment and the dangers which threaten the natural environment, can be solved only through patient negotiations for the definition and execution of a series of measures on matters of armament and weapons control and also the correct use of raw materials, which now are evaluated as ammunition. These raw materials must be dedicated to economic and social development and the protection of human rights and freedom.

62. S.I. considers that there could not be a better monument to comrade Olaf Palme than the restoration of the right to live in peace, freedom and solidarity.

4. Peripheral Conflicts

63. Some of the toughest battles for liberation are going on in Latin America and the Carribean. We want peace in this area. We request the right of national self determination and sovereignty and respect for the principle of non involvment. We accept the concrete proposals which are included in those approved by the convention of Latin America and the Carribean, decisions which include these principles.

64. The Middle East is a battle field of tough conflicts which lead not only to the involvement of the governments of the countries concerned but also the superpowers. The activities of the forces which are fighting each other prevent the restoration of peace on a national and international scale, and prevent the stopping of loss of life.

65. S.I. applauds the intentions of countries, members of the organisation, who during their visit to Israel intend to make a great effort to ensure a continuous peace in the area. S.I. considers that this can be done only through political negotiations between the interested parties, which must include the legal representatives of the Palestinian people. Peace must be secured on the basis of the common right of these countries to live in peace and security according to defined borders and to the right of the Palestinian people to live in their own country. This prerequires mutual respect between Arabs and Jews and the stop of all violence.

66. S.I. takes into consideration the role of U.N. and every other organisation which contributes to the success of this effort. S.I. expresses its deep concern at the continuous undermining of efforts made to restore the right and steady peace in the Middle East. S.I. asserts its belief that peace in the area and between people who live there, can only be established through the patient study of other possibilitities of cohabitation between Israel, the Palestinian people and their Arab neighbours. Supporting the people of that area, S.I. invites all countries to examine this problem; also the U.N. should seek for a solution through political dialogue for the stopping of violence and terrorism and the creation of positive conditions for peace.

67. S.I. expresses its concern about the existence of encampments in the occupied areas, despite international law and U.N. enactments, which is a fact that reduces the possibilities of negotiations.

68. The way to peace is long and difficult. S.I. judges the proposals of the Simon Peres government as positive and useful. We also keep in mind the Arabic proposal at Fez.

69. Since the last convention of 1983 the increasing suffering of the Lebanese people, of the Palestinian refugees who sought asylum there and other victims of terrorism are continuing terrible facts. S.I. affirms its decisive support for the sovereignty, the integrity and the unity of this country. S.I. calls upon all Lebanese to unite on a common program of national reconstruction and development and the establishment of democratic powers which is the only way to restore peace and to reject terrorism and violence. S.I. considers that the complete withdrawal of all foreign armies from Lebanese territory will help to decrease the enormous tension in the country.

70. S.I. voted for a decision to the Cypriot problem during the meeting of the Office in April 1984, and sent two representatives to the island – (the last one in August 1984), Now S.I. reaffirms approval of its members decision on the problem of Cyprus, and appeals for immediate withdrawal of the Turkish occupation in accordance with the U.N. decisions regarding Cyprus

and fully supports the efforts of the U.N.'s General Secretary to arrange this matter.

71. S.I. expresses its anxiety about the war between Iran-Iraq, which has been going on for six years. The conflict between these countries threatens security in the area and causes huge loss of human lives and threatens the economy of both countries which are deviating from the course of devlopment. S.I. in accordance with the actions of its departed vice-President Olaf Palme, condemns all violations of the Geneva agreement relating to the prohibition of toxic weapons and in respect of veteran's rights and invites the two countries to cease war and to declare peace on the basis of these agreements and of international guaranties for non-involvement in the internal problems of the two countries who should be free to choose the form of their own government. We support the U.N.'s efforts, the Independent Countries Organisation and the Islamic Conference, and all of those who fight for peace.

72. The future peace and security of Asia and the Pacific Ocean depends on the restoration of stable and democratic political forms of government in the Philippines and Korea.

73. In relation with that, S.I. greets the new democratic government of the Philippines. The declaration of 'People's Authority' made possible a useful political reformation. S.I. believes that President Coracon Acino will succeed in restoring a strong democratic system to the country on the basis of successful economic reformation.

74. S.I. considers that the continuing efforts towards democratic reformation in South Korea, and the increase of democratic forces in these difficult conditions, are encouraging.

75. S.I. supports all efforts to find new ways of easing withdrawal of the Vietnamese army from Cambodia.

76. We reaffirm our opposition to apartheid to NAD as made clear at the special conference of Arusa, Tanzania in September 1984 and at the extra meeting of S.I. in Gaborone, Botswana in April 1986. No one can compromise with apartheid. Apartheid must be eliminated. Apartheid cannot be revived.

77. We regard the African National Congress, the United democratic front, the syndicates and all the progressive powers whatever their race, to be a hope of NAD and of humanity in general. We positively condemn the recent activities of NAD against Botswana, Zimbabwe and Zambia.

78. NAD continues to destabilise the situation and to act illegally towards these countries. It is aiming to weaken their strength and to draw them into bloody conflict by every means, including military activities

against neighbouring countries. NAD Is ready to sacrifice the lives of people and the economy and also the refugees, in order to become master of the land.

79. Socialist International considers that Namibia has to be freed immediately, according to enactment 435 of U.N. There is no other solution for a really independent Namibia. There is no doubt that SUADO is the main representative of Namibia. It is not right for someone to examine both on one hand Nambia's independence and on the other hand the possible withdrawal of the Cuban Army. The support of UNITA in Angola only complicates the issue and in reality means nothing more than support of South African oppression in Namibia.

80. Taking the opportunity of the 10th anniversary of Soveto's uprising in 1976, the South African government took suppressive measures and used force, declaring a state of emergency. The natives are victims of plain terrorism. NAD continues to destabilise the situation and attacks the neighbouring countries. The whole world bears the responsibility for not putting a stop to this tough policy.

81. International sanctions are maybe the last resort to bring about peaceful reformations. The political opposition of NAD supports these measures. That's why S.I. calls on everyone to:
– Stop any investment in NAD and also loans to the government
– Impose a constant embargo on oil from the producing countries in order to prohibit exports and their conveyance from NAD and also to impose an embargo on the exports of coal from NAD
– To stop all aerial and sea trade with NAD
– To prohibit the imports of South African agricultural products.

82. If organisations like the U.N. and the E.E.C. cannot decide a policy of real penalties against the NAD the individual countries should undertake independent actions.

83. S.I. also supports the right of the Sahara people to self deter-mination and independence. We affirm our support to the opening of negotiations between the POLISARIO front and Morocco to find fair and final solution of this conflict.

84. S.I. believes that the struggle of Eritrea's people for self deter-mination which has been going on for 30 years must find a solution according to U.N.'s proposals and O.A.K.

85. S.I. expresses its deep concern for the perplexing military occupation of Afghanistan by the Soviet Union. S.I. is also concerned about the violations of human rights by the Soviet Union and by the Kamboul's government troops against both the resistance forces and the ordinary

population, also for the four million Afghanian refugees to Pakistan and Iran. S.I. supports the U.N.'s efforts to find a political solution to this problem, which naturally should be based on the withdrawal of Soviet troops and the restoration of people's rights to self-determination. S.I. calls on all the countries-members of this organisation – to offer help to the Afghan people, both to the refugee encampment and to the country itself.

86. We are deeply concerned about the continuing violations of human rights, and especially about actions against the final enactment of Helsinki which is related to the freedom of humans and ideas. That's why we express our solidarity for whoever is fighting for freedom, for collective rights, for religious freedom or for the protection of national minorities. We believe that if we dedicate our forces to the struggle for disarmament and the decrease of tension, favourable conditions for the achievement of ideals will be created.

87. In the meanwhile S.I. well understands that the life style of the Jews in USSR gets progressively worse and specifically the prohibition of Russian Jews from leaving the country independently in their desire to go to Israel. We also understand the increasing worries of those Jews who are seeking their (acceptable to all) rights to move out. We appeal to the Soviet Union to free those Jews who are imprisoned just for their efforts to acquire an exit visa and to allow all Jews who want to leave the USSR to do so without further problems. It is sad also that the Soviet authorities refuse to allow the Jews the right to learn and teach their mother-tongue.

88. We have talked about death and destruction, about the violation of human rights and the restriction of economic growth as the general outcome of peripheral conflicts. It is better, now, to finish this short and selected review with more concrete observations. In Northern Ireland terrorism, death and destruction disrupt everyday life. The signed British-Irish agreement between the governments of the United Kingdom and Ireland should be taken as positive and could help bring about stability and the complete cessation of conflict by respecting the political and cultural traditions of Ireland. Both governments and the parties of the United Kingdom, Northern Ireland and the Irish Republic are worthy of full support in their efforts to secure peace and harmony. Specifically European Socialists can offer their assistance for the solution of the deep economic crisis in Northern Ireland.

5. From Geneva to Lima

89. In 1976, in Geneva, when Willy Brandt became the leader of S.I. we decided to dedicate our powers to the creation of a World's organisation. We

didn't fully succeed in our purpose, but we can claim with pride that more than any other movement, we succeeded in what we had set out to do.

90. We can't however say that we are completely happy. We must double our efforts to create general global progressive forces. Until then we hope to restore other aims – like mutual relations with the new labour and socialist parties in the small islands of the Atlantic coasts.

91. When we work to perfect Lima's declaration of our new principles we should remember our successes as well as our failures.

92. In the frame work of our international organisation we believe that the creation of a movement for women will enable us to go ahead in the reformation of the organisation, and show our respect for a great part of our members and voters. This initiative will be approved by all woman around the world. As a proof of our stead fast decision we must follow the example of a great number of the countries, members of the S.I., who have given a large percentage of their resources to encourage the participation of women in leading associations. These percentages are between 15 and 50 per cent, the best number depending on the extent of women's participation.

93. The world's program of activity during the second half of the 'decade dedicated to women' as it was declared by the U.N., shows a willingness to promote the participation of women in political administrations. S.I. calls upon all member countries to offer their help in the creation of an organisation, or rather a Ministry, which will execute the programs which will secure equality between men and women. S.I. also calls upon all member countries to make it easy for women to participate in political life as equal partners of men and to ensure that there is a women's committee at every level of administration as, for instance, the candidature for local, national or peripheral elections.

94. S.I. declares that they will support the proposals put forward for the 'Socialist decade of the women', which was acclaimed at the convention of women – members of S.I. in Lima.

95. We are obligated to include these articles in Lima's Manifest, also the declaration which publicises the first convention of S.I. in a Third World country.

96. Once again S.I. reaffirms from Lima its resolve to work for the fulfilment of the dream of a world in which people live peacefully, freely and in unity with each other.

Mid-Atlanti: Res:arch Associates, Inc.

Directors:
Robert Moss
Arnaud de Borchgrave
John Rees

Confidential

THE SOCIALIST INTERNATIONAL

January 3, 1985

©1985

P.O. Box 1523, Washington, D.C. 20013
1-800-638-2086; in Maryland. 301-366-2531

Το εξώφυλλο της απόρρητης έκθεσης που συντάχθηκε κατ᾽ εντολή και με έξοδα της ΣΙΑ για τη Σοσιαλιστική Διεθνή, από ειδικό αμερικανικό γραφείο.

The confidential document of CIA for the Socialist International.

8

A Confidential Report about Socialist International made at the expense of the C.I.A.

The concern of the USA and more particularly of their secret agency about Socialist Internation has been further revealed by a confidential report about the latter made at the expense of the C.I.A. The report was executed by the American Research Office M.A.R.A. (Mid Atlantic Research Associates Inc.), P.O. Box 1523, Washington D.C. 20013 Tel. 800–638–2086 and Maryland 301–366–2531.

The report entitled THE SOCIALIST INTERNATIONAL, dated 3 January 1985 and described as confidential consists of a summary and six chapters.

The complete text of the above Report is given below to help the reader to form an opinion about current thinking in the United States regarding Socialist International.

EXECUTIVE SUMMARY

• The Socialist International (SI), a forum for debate and policy co-ordination among many of the world's socialist and social democratic parties, is expected to increase its active role in opposition to U.S. policies in Central America and Southern Africa, and in support of U.S. arms control agreements with the Soviet Union that would among other things halt U.S. development of strategic defense systems against in-flight missiles.

• A White House meeting with President Reagan in April or May is expected to boost the international prestige of SI president Willy Brandt, and *enhance his efforts to make himself a principal intermediary between the U.S. and the USSR.* Brandt, chairman of the West German Social Democratic Party (SPD), was forced, to resign as chancellor when one of his closest aids, Gunther Guillaume, was discovered to be an East German intelligence officer. Brandt, given an effusive welcome in Havana last fall, has never deviated from his 'Ostpolitik' efforts.

• The Socialist International is expanding its operations in Latin America and Africa, with an outreach program to militant parties who lack the

59

electoral traditions of European social democracy. In *Southern Africa, this includes SI support for the 'Frontline' states* and Soviet-armed and trained terrorist forces against South Africa. In Latin America, the *SI's affiliates and associates include the political wings of the Soviet and Cuban-supported guerrilla movements* in El Salvador and Guatemala, the Sandinistas, and other parties who work in a 'secret regional caucus' of the SI under the direction of the Americas Department of the Cuban Communist Party Central Committee.

• Anti-Communist social democratic parties in the SI still form a vocal minority, but they lack the financial and political resources of Brandt's SPD, the British Labour Party and other major parties which support rapprochement with the Soviets and Soviet surrogates, particularly in the Third World.

CONTENTS

Executive Summary
1. Socialists and the Third World.
2. Rio Bureau Meeting.
3. Arusha Conference.
4. Background.
5. SI in the U.S.
6. Organisation.

1. Socialists and the Third World.

The Socialist International (SI), a forum for debate and coordination among many of the world's socialist and social democratic parties, has been influential in exacerbating a trend among socialist parties in which their former strong stand against cooperation with the communist parties and the Soviet Union has weakened, sometimes dramatically. As a result particularly in the Third World, the Socialist International has been encouraging in an active manner Soviet surrogates hostile to Western democracy as a whole, and to the interests of the United States in particular.

The sharply leftward course of Western Europe's Socialist and Social Democratic parties is one of the more significant political developments of the last fifteen years. During the first three decades after World War II. Western Europe's major political parties agreed to a basic and general consensus on defense which was not fundamentally challenged despite differences among the varied nations that comprise the North Atlantic

Treaty Organization. This held whether the governing parties were conservatives, Christian democratics, social democrats or socialists. Since a major reorganization of the Socialist International in 1976, the formerly Euro-centric organization has reached out to recruit new members among Third World parties. Yet many of those parties come from a revolutionary tradition alien to European social democracy and its fundamental parliamentarism. *In 1983, a secret caucus of Central American* and Caribbean leftist SI members met in secret with Cuba's 'active measures' chief, *Manuel Pineiro Losada,* a member of the Cuban Communist Party Central Committee, and chief of its Americas Department, to coordinate tactics before a key SI meeting.

Recent Socialist International meetings in Rio de Janeiro and Arusha, Tanzania, demonstrate that very obviously the trend to the left is continuing and is being intensified.

2. Rio Bureau Meeting

The SI Bureau meeting in Rio de Janeiro, October 1–2, 1984, confirmed the Willy Brandt groups commitment to closer ties with the Sandinistas, the Farabundo Marti National Liberation Front/Revolutionary Democratic Front (FMLN/FDR) and Fidel Castro.

The Central America focus of the Bureau meeting was to persuade the FSLN to agree to cosmetic changes that would allow opposition leader Arturo Cruz to run for president and ensure a broader acceptance by world public opinion of the November elections as legitimate. Among those involved in working out the arrangement were *Carlos Andres Perez, Mario Soares; Hans-Jurgen Wischnewski of the SPD Presidium; Dieter Koniesen, a personal adviser to Brandt; and SPD foreign relations secretary, Hans-Eberhard Dingels.* Despite their efforts, FSLN Comandante Beyardo Arce Castano and his Aides from the FSLN International Relations Department – deputy chief José Pasos Liarsiag Raul Guerra, South American section chiefs and West European chief Herman Estrada –*walked out of the SI Bureau meeting.* They refused to allow Cruz a four-day voter registration extention period in which he could consult with his supporters, and would not agree to not harrass and disrupt opposition political campaigning. (Even without that, Cruz received about 30 percent of the votes).

The Sandinista refusal to accept democratic electoral norms did not inhibit Brandt from visiting Managua and Havana after the Bureau meeting. Indeed, in Havana, Fidel Castro accorded Brandt a reception suitable for a visiting head of state. Brandt appeared charmed as he was during a similarly warm meeting with Leonid Brezhnev four years before. Yet it cannot be doubted that Brandt and other SI officials know the contents of minutes captured following the October 1983 U.S. invasion of Grenada which recorded the activities of a secret caucus of radical Latin American and Caribbean SI parties led by the Cuban Communist Party's 'active measures' chief, Manuel Pinelro Losada, formerly the chief of the *Direccion General de Inteligencia* (DGI).

As one critic of the SI noted, 'in the entire stream of SI denunciations of Chile, Argentina, Guatemala, Paraguay, Uruguay and Honduras, there has *never* been an SI condemnation of Castroism, (and) *never* a call for pluralism in Cuba'.

A cover letter from Pineiro 'with revolutionary best wishes' provided leaders of Grenada's New JEWEL Movement (NJM) with details of the June 1981 meeting in Managua of the Socialist International Committee for the Defense of the Revolution in Nicaragua, created on the initiative of Brandt at the 15th SI Congress in November 1980. Among the Cuban documents found in Grenada was a lengthy analysis of the Socialist International from the Communist perspective. It noted:

'The 13th Congress of the SI, held in Geneva in 1976, considered the new changes that were taking place in the projection and relations of Social Democracy with the so-called Third World, especially Latin America and the Caribbean...'

Noting that eight Latin American and Caribbean parties were added to the SI at that meeting, the Cubans remarked:

'It should be stressed that the documents adopted did not contain the traditional formulations of obstinate anticommunism... that had characterized SI's stand,... Besides, the so-called 'democratic socialism'... was not stressed as an 'alternative project' between capitalism and communism; a certain flexibility of the stubborn stand concerning relations with other communist parties and progressive forces took place'.

Of particular significance, in the opinion of the Cubans, was an April 1980 solidarity conference with the Sandinistas organized by the *SI-related Center for Democratic Studies on Latin America* (CEDAL) in Costa Rica attended by representatives of 19 parties. In the conference resolutions, 'imperialism was condemned and denounced by name;' 'the need for unity of the left in every country' was recognized; and the need to spread the Nicaraguan struggle to 'other Latin American peoples such as Guatemala and El Salvador' was 'literally stated'.

The analysis sent to the New JEWEL Movement leaders by Pineiro concluded that the Socialist International had a 'dual nature'. Though on the one hand, a rival of the communists' essential objectives:

'On the other, it is obvious that certain political positions of Social Democracy can be used by the revolutionary and progressive forces of the continent at given junctures of the struggle against the repressive and fascist military regimes and of the confrontation with U.S. imperialism'.

The 'Secret Regional Caucus' which held its meetings in Grenada included a representative of the Cuban Communist Party identified as Silva, Antonio Marguin of the Sandinstas, Hector Oqueli of the MNR of El Salvador, Paul Miller of the People's National Party (PNP) of Jamaica, a representative of the Radical Party of Chile identified as Freda, and Chris DeRiggs of Grenada's NJM.

With the *SI's Chile Committee co-chaired by Alex Kitson of Great Britain* who during a visit to Moscow had proclaimed that he felt more at home in the USSR than he did in his own country (as well he might since his father was a leader of the South African Communist Party and the terrorism campaign initiated in the early 1960s by the ANC and served some twenty years in prison before being released and deported to Britain recently) indications are that the SI will continue to work to thwart U.S. policy in Latin America and the Caribbean, and to destabilize U.S.-allied governments in Southern Africa and Latin America.

3. Arusha Conference.

The Socialist International's southern Africa involvements were also considered by the 'Secret Regional Caucus'. The SI has taken a position strongly *supportive of two Soviet surrogate terrorist organizations, the African National Congress (ANC) and South West Africa People's Organization (SWAPO).*

On September 4, a two-day meeting on political development in Southern Africa opened in Arusha, Tanzania, sponsored by the Socialist International's Committee on Southern Africa. In this meeting the SI's European members joined with leaders of the 'front-line' started to work out ways of supporting the ANC and SWAPO guerrillas, and to undermine south Africa.

The Arusha meeting was the occasion of a quarrel between the political faction led by Swedish Prime Minister Olaf Palme, and 'moderates' led by Portuguese Prime Minister Mario Soares *The source of the quarrel was Soares' (and Mozambique's) argument that the SI parties should talk to*

South Africa and try to persuade Pretoria to come to an accommodation with the terrorists. In contrast, Palme and the Radicals argued that the Socialists should concentrate on supporting ANC and SWAPO. Both factions agreed to support the groups involved in 'armed struggle' and to provide assistance to the 'front-line' states which harbour them.

While Sweden has expanded trade relations with South Africa, Palme appears to be focusing on ways to establish a climate for violent insurrection in the form of a race war in South Africa. Palme was reported to have been the individual who led the campaign to have the Nobel Committee select Episcopal Bishop Desmond Tutu as the 1984 Nobel Peace Prize laureat.

In addition to Palme and Soares, participants in the Arusha meetings included Tanzanian President Julius Nyerere, accompanied by Prime Minister Salim Ahmed Salim; Botswana's President Quett Masire, with Assistant Minister of Agriculture Mathaba Phirl; Mozambique's President Samora Liachel with Foreign Affairs Minister Joequim Chissano, Information Minister Jose Luis Cabaco, and Security Minister Sergio Vieira; Zimbabwean Prime Minister Robert Mugabe; Portugal's foreign, trade, treasury and cooperation ministers, the deputy governor of the Bank of Portugal, and a number of parliamentarians; Lionel Justin, Secretary General of the French Socialist Party; Zambian President Kenneth Khaunda; Sam Nujoma, president of SWAPO; ANC president Nough Oliver Tambo; Pascoal Luvualy from Angola's MPLA–The Angolan Workers' Party Politburo: and Major General Joseph Garba, chairman of the U.N. Committee for Action Against Apartheid, as well as the SI parties from Belgium, Denmark, Finland, Italy, Holland and Norway.

Among the resolutions was a call for total adherence to an embargo of military-related trade with South Africa. But, significantly, the SI leaders from Belgium, Denmark, Finland, France, the Netherlands, Norway, Austria, Portugal, Spain, Sweden, West Germany and the United Kingdom avoided naming the countries which are collaborating in the military field with Pretoria. Two of the West German SPD officials who attended the Arusha meeting, Bremen's Lord Mayor Hans Koschnick and Gunter Verheugen, spokesman for the SPD on Southern African affairs argued that a militantly pro-ANC position was essential because economic and racial progress in South Africa was merely 'stabilizing apartheid' Verneugen also put considerable effort into condemning South Africa for linking their withdrawal from Namibia to Cuban withdrawal from Angola, apparently quite unaware that the 'Linkage' initiative was an American invention.

SI relations with Third World guerrilla groups are extensive, as indicated by the inclusion among the official observers at the April, 1983 SI congress in Portugal of FDR of El Salvador; three Eritrean guerrilla groups fighting for independence from Ethiopia; the National Revolutionary Unity of Guatemala (URNG), which includes an armed faction of the pro-Moscow Communist Party; the ANC: Palestine Liberation Organization. (PLO); POLISARIO: and three Marxist-Leninist ruling parties – Nicaragua's FSLN Mozambique's FRELIMO and the MLAWP (Movement for the Liberation of Angola-Workers Party) of Angola.

4. Background.

The Socialist International traces its ancestry to the International Working-men's Association (First International) formed in 1864 in London by Karl Marx which was dissolved in 1874; and to the Second or Socialist International founded in 1889 in Brussels by Friedrich Engels which collapsed in 1914 under political and ideological pressures arising from the outbreak of the First World War.

The present SI was oranized in 1951 at a conference in Frankfurt, West Germany. The Frankfurt declaration rejected 'uncontrolled' and 'mono-polistic' capitalism, but also attacked Communism, stating that 'Communism has split the international labor movement'; that 'inter-national Communism is the instrument of a new imperialism', and that 'wherever it has achieved power it has destroyed freedom or the chance of gaining freedom'.

The post-war SI leaders proclaimed:

'Democratic socialists recognize the maintenance of world peace as the supreme task in our time. Peace can be secured only by a system of collective security. This will create the conditions for international disarmament'.

Meeting in 1962 in Oslo, the SI was still harshly critical of the Soviet Union and Communism, declaring that:

'They (USSR) now claim to base their foreign policy on the principles of peaceful coexistence. In practice, however, this is only a change of tactics, and the struggle against the non-communist world is continued in a different form.... East-West rivalry has largely been imposed upon an unwilling world by the communist leaders. Although the communist countries claim to be peace-loving, the way in which they have used their military power has aggravated tension in the world'.

However, in some sectors of the SI, a change in outlook towards the Communists amounting to taking an opposite position became visible at the end of the next year. Leading this change were two leaders of the West

German SPD – Egon Sahr, the originator and Willy Brandt, the popularizer, of 'Ostpolitik'. When Brandt became Chancellor of the Federal Republic of Germany (FRG), he instituted coexistence policies as 'change through rapprochement'.

The British Labour party and the proverbially 'Finlandized' Finnish Social Democratic Party also persistently urged that the SI adopt 'detente' with the Communists. The Finnish SDP promoted the concept that to promote 'dialogue', the SI parties should institute party-to-party relations with local Communist parties and with the Communist Party of the Soviet Union (CPSU).

At the SI's 11th Congress in Eastbourne in June 1969 the attitude of the SI to relations with the Communists had become clear. The resolution spoke about the totalitarian nature of Communism, but dropped the Oslo declaration's understanding that 'peaceful coexistence' meant 'struggle against the non-communist parties which considered collaborating with Communists in electoral or governing coalitions. The former emphasis on maintaining a credible military deterrent was replaced by priorities of disarmament and human rights. Both themes became key to increased Socialist ties and collaboration with the Communist parties during the 1970s.

With the institution of U.S.–Soviet *detente* during the Nixon Administration, the Soviets moved on the SI, obviously as one mechanism for influencing the climate of opinion in the European Socialist parties. The Soviet outreach to the SI, in which Mikhail Suslov in the Politburo, Yuri Andropov at the KGB, and CPSU International Department chief Boris Ponomarev were central, can be viewed as one element in a multi-level Soviet 'active measures' campaign to deceive and lull the West during a critical period in which the Soviets expected thirty years of weapons research and development to bear fruit.

Specialists on Soviet policy see the USSR's overall program as having a number of elements, among them:

• proclaiming 'peaceful coexistence' which placed a premium on 'active measures' deceptions of Western political leaders and public opinion makers; subversion; and cover support to surrogates and clients in the Third World.

• arms control negotiations aimed at hindering and impeding the flow of Western strategic military developments.

• subversion of anti-communism as a principle of Western political parties, trade union international organizations and other institutions.

In a 1971 article in the CPSU journal, *Kommunist,* Ponomarev wrote, 'The struggle against the social democratic ideology and policy remains a major task of the CPSU and the entire communist movement'. He explained that the USSR's 'new suggestions for unity' with socialists was part of a calculated 'unity' manoeuvre. Reminding the ideologically inflexible that 'Our party does not implement random international measures', Ponomarev wrote that 'It would be entirely justified to consider them as the expanded foreign political offensive' related to 'peace and the security of the peoples', meaning military questions. (emphasis added)

To reinforce these overtures, in that same year, CPSU general secretary, Leonid Brezhnev confirmed the new policy, proclaiming the CPSU's readiness 'to develop cooperation with the social democrats'.

The speed of the SI's move to the left escalated dramatically after Willy Brandt was forced to resign as West German Chancellor. Brandt's friend and closest advisor, Gunther Guillaume, was revealed to be an East German agent. Still, Brandt's friends in the SPD leadership saw no reason to remove him from that post; and one of these, Egon Bahr, appears to have taken on the 'Guillaume role' in Brandt's inner circle.

Brandt became increasingly active in the SI. By 1975, he had taken charge and at the Geneva congress in 1976, persuaded the SI to institute 'reforms' in the name of 'revitalization'. This meant recruiting Third World socialist parties although quite a number of them lacked the tradition of electoral democracy of the European parties. As Bernt Carlsson, general secretary from 1976 to 1983, noted at the 1983 *Lisbon* Congress:

'a majority of our membership is now non-European. The major focus of our activities was peace and disarmament. The Socialist International... attempted to act upon the words of President Brandt, that 'we are, above all, the worldwide party of peace'. The Socialist International Disarmament and Arms Control Advisory Council, established at the Madrid congress, undertook missions to both superpowers and to the UN, under the directorship of Kalevi Sorsa and Walter Hacker. And, in an activity undertaken outside the international but paralleling our work. Olaf Palme chaired the Independent Commission on Disarmament and Security Issues....

'The greatest increase in our activity in this inter-congress period, as compared to previous years, came in the Latin American/Caribbean area.

'The attempt to find a negotiated and just settlement in El Salvador has been an important focus of our activity. The International has also worked hard in supporting other parties suffering under dictatorship, such as those in Guatemala and Chile....

'The International has also played an active role in support of the project of the Nicaraguan revolution – and actively resisted all attempts by foreign forces to interfere with the course of that revolution....

'The international has devoted considerable energy to the questions of Southern Africa, and will continue to do so in the next inter-congress period....

'In South Africa, the policy of apartheid continues to take its toll – Nelson Mandela is still in jail, Neil Aggett died in jail, and the suppression of the majority of the population continues.... We have continued our support for SWAPO and the ANC (African National Congress) and the Black Consciousness Movement and for the frontline states, and have asked member parties to make every effort to reduce their nation's economic links with the minority regime in South Africa'.

Indeed, the chairman of the Socialist International's Disarmament Council (SIDAC), Finnish Prime Minister, Kalevi Sorsa, has taken an aggressive role in urging that the SI become the intermediary between the United States and the Soviets. Prior to the announcement that U.S.–Soviet arms control talks would resume this month. Sorsa chaired a SIDAC planning session in Tokyo. He announced that he planned to meet with both the U.S. and Soviet leaders in April or May on arms control issues. However, Sorsa and SIDAC has been preempted by SI president Willy Brandt, who will be the one to have a White House audience with President Reagan. However, in matters of arms control and other issues, there is little to choose between the champion of 'Ostpolitik' and the Prime Minister of a country whose name has become synonymous with cowed, enforced 'neutrality'. Still, as chairman of SIDAC, Sorsa will sponsor a major disarmament conference this fall in Finland which a substantial Soviet delegation will attend.

5. SI in the U.S.

The larger of two U.S. affiliates of the Socialist International is the Democratic Socialists of America (DSA), based at 853 Broadway, Suite 801, New York, NY 10003 (212/260-3270). DSA emerged in 1981 from the merger of the new American Movement (NAM) and Democratic Socialist Organizing Committee (DSOC). NAM was an expression of 'Euro-communism' that emerged in 1970 from former members of Students for a

Democratic Society (SDS) and disillusioned ex-members of the Communist Party, U.S.A. DSOC, led by Michael Harrington, was a full member of the Socialist international, active, despite its small size, in the sector moving towards rapprochement with the Communist left and Soviet Third World surrogates.

Through merger with NAM, the U.S. democratic socialists accepted an influential group of veteran Communist Party organizers and activists who broke party discipline following the 1966 invasion of Czechoslovakia, and who have since been advocates of the European Communist-Socialist rapprochement. The leading spokesman for that tendency is Dorothy Healey, a DSA vice-chair. Her son, Richard, now on the staff of a radical lobbying organization in Washington, the Coalition for a New Foreign and Military Policy (CNFMP), was NAM's national secretary and is active in the DSA leadership.

DSA's leadership has multiple links with organizations linked to Soviet 'active measures' operations. For example, DSA vice-chair Edwin Vargas, vice-president of the Connecticut Federation of Teachers, is a council member of the Soviet-controlled World Peace Council (WPC). DSA vice-chairs include Rep. Ronald V. Dellume (D-CA); Frances Boore Lappe, co-director of the Institute for Food and Development Policy (IFDP); Manning Marable; and D.C. City Council Member Hilda Mason, all of whom have links with Washington's thinktank of the pro-Soviet left, the Institute for Policy Studies (IPS). Other DSA vice-chairs include San Francisco's avowed homosexual supervisor Harry Britt; Irving Howe; Marjorie Phyfe; Christine Riddlough; theologian Rosemary Reuther; and William Winpisinger, the flamboyant president of the International Association of Machinists (IAM).

Traditionally, DSA and DSOC have operated as a caucus within the Democratic Party, pressing for what DSA's critics on the left have termed 'a New Deal type of Keynesian economics and some form of social control over corporate decisions'.

In International issues such as solidarity with the Central American insurgents and the Sandinistas, DSA's alignment with the Marxist-Leninist left is visible. DSA co-chairs Harrington and Barbara Ehrenreich see the 1985 priority as 'expanding our peace and Central America work' and remaining active in the 'anti-war and anti-nuclear arms movements'. This was viewed essentially as partisan oppositionism – playing 'a major role in struggles against oncoming Reagan initiatives, foreign and domestic' no matter what the issue, 'in preparation for the emergence of the popular left in the Democratic Party in '86 and '88'.

In December 1980, as the Reagan forces were about to take office, the DSA demonstrated its influence in the left wing of the Democratic Party with a Washington conference sponsored by its tax-exempt arm, the Institute for Democratic Socialism (IDS). Some 2,500 people attended meetings 'Eurosocialism and America', among them U.S. activists and Foreign Socialist International luminaries. Among them were Socialist trade union leaders and parliamentarians including SI president Willy Brandt, leader of West Germany's Social Democratic Party (SPD); SI General Secretary Brent Carlsson; Tony Been and Clive Jenkins of the British Labour Party; José Francisco Pena Gómez, leader of the *Partido Revolucionario Dominicano* (PRD) (Dominican Revolutionary Party). The chief U.S. celebrity slated to participate, Senator Edward Kennedy (D-MA), did not appear, but instead, held a private dinner with the SI leaders and former Senator George McGovern.

However, the European Socialist leaders recognized long ago that neither DSOC nor the SDUSA were major national political forces in the U.S. For many years, the Socialist leaders including Olaf Palme of Sweden, Bruno Kreisky of Austria and Willy Brandt, held informal meetings during August at the town of Harpsund on the coast of Sweden. The compatible U.S. political leader selected as a regular participant was Senator Hubert Humphrey. But when Humphrey became Vice President in 1965, he felt his continued participation in the Harpsund meetings was politically ill-advised. Thus he designated as his replacement his protege, Walter Mondale, then aged 37 and Minnosota's new Senator.

Expert sources on the SI maintain that Palme and Mondale developed a close personal and political friendship in which Palme was instrumental in informing Mondale about foreign affairs issues, particularly those in Southern Africa and Latin America. They also say that the close relationship between Mondale and Palme continued through the 1984 presidential campaign, with Swedish U.N. Ambassador Andera Fer acting as intermediary.

5. SI Organization.

The SI Secretarial maintains modest offices in the United Kingdom at 88a St. John's Wood High Street, London NW8 7SJ. Under its president, Willy Brandt, the SI organization has twenty-five vice presidents and a General Secretary who coordinates international activities. The SI General Secretary (who replaced Bernt Carlsson in 1983) is Pentti Vaananen of the Finnish Social Democratic Party, a labor lawyer who, as the Finnish SDP's

International Secretary since 1976, has been a leader of disarmament activities.

The SI Vice-Presidents include:

Ichio Asukota, Japan.

Ed Broadbent, New Democratic Party (NDP), Canada.

Bettino Crazi, Socialist Party of Italy (Prime Minister).

Michael Foot, Labour Party Britain.

Felipe Gonsalez, Socialist Workers Party of Spain (PSOE) (Prime Minister).

Bob Hawke, Australian Labour Party (Prime Minister).

Anker Joergensen, Social Democratic Party of Denmark.

Lionel Jospin, Socialist Party of France.

Walid Jumblatt, Progressive Socialist Party of Lebanon (and member of the Presidential Committee of the Soviet-controlled World Peace Council (WPC)).

Bruno Kreisky, Socialist Party of Austria.

Michael Manley, People's National Party of Jamaica.

Daniel Oduber, National Liberation Party (PLN) of Costa Rica.

Olaf Palme, Social Democratic Party of Sweden (Prime Minister).

José Francisco Pena Gomez, Dominican Revolutionary Party (PRD).

Shimon Peres, Israel Labor Party (Prime Minister).

Carlos Andrés Pérez, *Acclón Democratica* of Venezuela.

Irene Patry, Belgian Socialist Party.

Lydie Schmit, Socialist International Women.

Leopold Senghor, *Parti Socialiste Sengalaise.*

Mario Soares, Portuguese Socialist Party (Prime Minster).

Kalevi Sorsa, Social Democratic Party of Finland (Prime Minister).

Anselmo Sule, Radical Party of Chile.

Reiulf Steen, Norwegian Labor Party.

Guillermo Ungo, *Movimento Nacional Revolucionarlo* (MNR), part of the guerrilla FMLN/FDR.

Joop den Uyl, Netherlands Labor Party.

Other full member parties of the SI include the Barbados Labour Party; Belgian Socialist Party; Danish Social Democratic Party; Icelandic Social Democratic Party; Irish Labour Party; Israel's MAPAM Party; Italian Social Democratic Party; Japan Socialist Party (JSP); Japan Democratic Socialist Party (JDSP); (South) Korean (ROK) United Socialist Party; Luxembourg Socialist Workers Party; Malaysian Democratic Action Party; Malta Labour Party; Mauritius Labour Party; New Zealand Labour Party; Northern Ireland Labour Party; Northern Ireland Social

Democratic and Labour Party; Swiss Social Democratic Party; Turkish Republican People's Party; and the DSA and SDUSA of the United States.

The SI maintains other categories of affiliation: There are more than a dozen 'consultative' parties – among them the EDEK Socialist Party of Cyprus, the Febrerista Revolutionary Party of Paraguay; the Working People's Alliance (WPA) of Guyana; the *Alianza Popular Revolucionaria Amerciana* (APRA) of Peru; the Progressive Labour Party of St. Lucia; and the *Partido Independentista Puertorriquena* (PIP) (Puerto Rican Independence Party) led by Ruben Berrios.

c) Finance and Administration Committee, which is elected by the Bureau and is composed of representatives of seven SI parties and fraternal organizations, meets two or three times a year.

d) Secretariat, supervised by the SI General Secretary, prepares agendas, budget estimates, agendas for SI meetings, and frequently participates in missions, study groups and meetings.

It should be emphasised that the main work of the SI is carried out through the member parties, which keeps the SI's organizational budget and staff relatively modest. Available figures indicate that the 1981 budget totalled £5706,350. Half of which went for a staff of eight and office costs of the London secretariat. Member parties are responsible for their own travel and participation in meetings. The parties paying the main dues assessments are the West German SPD £111,000; Swedish Social Democratic Party, $75,023; Austrian Socialist Party, $66,600; Italian Socialist Party (PSI), $37,000; British Labour Party, $30,525; Norwegian Labor Party, $25,900; Netherlands Labor Party, $22,866; and French Socialist Party, $22,200.

This does not give a true picture of SI resources. Much of the aid reportedly contributed to the Portuguese Socialist Party in the 1974–75 period, and that going to the Sandinista National Liberation Front (FSLN) in Nicaragua and Farabundo Marti Front in El Salvador actually is provided by individual parties, party foundations, and by the trade-union organizations associated with the individual parties.

For example, the Social Democratic Party (SPD) of West Germany, which provides the largest share of SI funds and is highly influential within the organization, operates through the Friedrich Ebert Foundation, which has been at the center of the SI's expansion of activities in Latin America.

The Socialist International is aggressively seeking to expand its influence in Latin America and Africa, and supports many policies parallel to those of the Soviet Union. The Soviets have long been conscious of the usefulness of the SI. Under the leadership of Boris Popnomarev, a candidate member of the Politburo and chief of the Committee, who was the first CPSU official to address a Socialist International Congress, relations between the SI and the Soviet Bloc parties continue to strengthen – though over the objections of anti-communist socialists who still comprise a substantial SI minority. In the field of arms control, the West German and Finnish social democratic parties are highly influential. Their influence is likely to increase with the prestige that is to be accorded Brandt via White House meetings later this year.

9

The Positions of S.I. and the Displeasure of the United States

The tension in the relations between Washington and Socialist International appeared from the very first day of S.I.'s existence. The principles of the program of S.I. are contained in the declaration 'For the purposes and duties of Democratic Socialism' which was approved at the Foundation Convention in Frankfurt, in May 1951. In the declaration it was pointed out that : 'Social democrats consider the establishment of ecumenical peace as the most important duty of our times'.

S.I. made a proposal to all countries for the establishment of peace, at a moment when White House policy had as 'a priority' exactly the opposite : That is the undermining of peace through the 'cold war' by every means they could and specially by the escalation of the arms race and the worsening of world tension. Washington not only followed that policy themselves but required the same from its allies in the different political or military coalitions.

Since the end of the '50's a trend has started to show in S.I.'s policy seeking a new political line, which found its most complete reflection in the British Labour Party's and West German Social Democratic Party's memoranda which included proposals for the creation of a zone of controlled armament in the centre of Europe and a system of collective security. These matters were examined in the Sixth Convention of S.I. in July 1959 in Hamburg. By the new proposals, European Social democrats were confronting the dogma of Washington, which still considers Europe to be a basic field of competition between East and West.

During the 60's and especially during the '70's many leaders of S.I. were appointed who favoured the principles of peaceful co-existence in order to unite all efforts in the struggle for peace. This attitude was reflected in the decisions of the synods of S.I.'s Council in Helsinki (May 1971) and the 12th Convention of S.I. in Vienna (June 1972). S.I.'s leaders supported the idea of arranging a conference for security and co-operation in Europe and they took an active part in its proceedings. During the '70's S.I. contributed significantly in the planning and application of political means to decrease tension and foster international cooperation, in Europe and outside.

This contrast between Washington and S.I. found a reflection in the manipulations of problems during the struggle for national liberation of people in Asia, Africa and Latin America. At the end of the '60's and the beginning of the '70's S.I. strongly supported the immediate stopping of the Vietnam War. Serious disagreements on how to handle the Middle East crisis errupted. In February 1973 in Chile (for the first time outside Europe) a session of the office of S.I. took place, in which it was evident that the organisation supported the struggle of Latin American people to achieve independence and social progress. In an extra session of the office of S.I. (September 1973) the military coup d'etat which was organised by the CIA was condemned.

For these exact facts the negative attitude of the White House towards S.I. becomes clear, especially after Ronald Reagan took over the presidency. More specifically this attitude of the U.S. was displayed to S.I.'s one representation which visited Washington at the end of October, 1981.

So, while in 1978 the representatives of S.I. had talked personally to Carter, in 1981 they just had meetings with an Undersecretary in the Ministry of Foreign Affairs, Pearl the Undersecretary in the Ministry of Defence, and the then Director of the Armament and Disarmament Control Agency, Rostow. From the very first day of their visit to the U.S. the representatives of S.I. realised that Americans are not overly concerned about the problems of disarmament. They also had to face imflammatory speeches, something that confirmed their fears regarding the prospects of further talks concerning the escalation of the arms race and the restoration of honest relations between S.I. and Reagan's administration.

The members of the representation departed for the U.S. with the intention of explaining to State officials in Washington all the disastrous results of the policy, imposed by the American government, of increasing armament and international tension. However, Pearl, the Undersecretary of Defence, didn't want to hear anything about the established facts put forward by the representatives in favour of a military and strategic balance between U.S. and U.S.S.R. Specifically surprising were Pearl's declarations regarding the policy of a nuclear war and the readiness of the U.S. to use neutron weapons.

On November 6, 1981, twelve representatives of S.I. broke off their talks in the Pentagon early, as a protest against the insulting behaviour of the clerks of the military services of the U.S.

In the report upon the activity of S.I. which was made by the White House especially for the President, it was suggested that American influence should be brought to bear on S.I.'s policy in order to eliminate any unfavourable results towards the U.S.

Washington dislikes the fact that S.I.'s leadership considers the struggle for disarmament to be one of its main objectives, and that they support a course leading towards disarmament and co-operation on a political and economic level with Moscow.

Intense anger was caused to the White House by the fact that S.I. did not agree with American assessments concerning the reasons for the appearance and escalation of the anti-war movement in West Europe and U.S., that S.I. supported Sandinistas leadership in Nicaragua and that it was opposed to the possibility of converting Nicaragua into a new Chile, that it condemned the American occupation of Grenada and the policy of supporting the bloody establishment in Salvador; also that it disagreed with Washington on the ways of dealing with conflicts in the Middle East, South Africa and other ares of the world.

As we will show in further sections of this book, not only the State Department and the Pentagon but also the CIA has started to undermine S.I.

Specifically CIA's activities followed these methods:
– Defamation of left wing forces and especially of the Socialdemocrat leaders, who criticized U.S. policy.
– Right wing forces taking over power and CIA's agents infiltrating the Socialdemocratic movement.
– Recruiting agents amongst the leaders of the correspondent parties.
– Undermining the Socialists positions, also control over their activity in order at the appropriate moment to cause rupture or elimination of the different parties.

We have to observe, on the other hand, that S.I. as a whole was faced from the start by the suspicions of not only the Republican but also the Democratic Party leaders in the U.S.A.

The hatred of both parties towards Democratic Socialism caused their negative attitude to S.I. The right wing conservative forces of the U.S.A. consider all Socialists to be Marxists whom nobody can trust or believe, and consider it is better for them to stay out of power. That's why in Washington they are backing the right wing conservative forces around the world, most especially in Europe.

The International Democratic Union

In one of his speeches which McDonald (a member of the house of representatives) gave in the U.S. Congress, he confessed that for many years

76

efforts had been made in Europe to confront S.I. with other political parties, which held pro-american opinions. In the European Congress, a European People's Party was established which joined the Christian democratic parties. Following that the European Democratic Union (EDU) was established, to which belong the conservative and Christiandemocratic parties of West Europe.

The year 1981 was a year of significant escalation in the European Democratic Union's activity against S.I. At the beginning of 1981 the office of EDU was considering the creation of a committee to deal with the problems of disarmament, as a counter-weight to the already established group which works in S.I.'s framework on the same matter.

According to those who wrote the report the existence of a team such as this would allow the conservatives to gain credit for participating in an examination of the problems standing in the way of peace and disarmament.

They also showed a special interest in recruiting new members from non European conservative parties. This is a remarkable fact, because exactly at the same time the U.S. expressed great interest in uniting worldwide, all conservative forces. For this reason the president of E.D.U., A. Mock, travelled in the Far East, Australia, New Zealand, Japan and also the Middle East. These visits of Mock were made at the same time as S.I. was interested in the Pacific Ocean area.

On June 26th, 1982 the peripheral part of EDU, the Democratic Union of Pacific Ocean, (DUPO), was created as a counter-weight to S.I.'s activity in that part of the world. The conservative parties of Australia, New Zealand and Japan joined the Union. Immediately after DUPO's creation, the leadership of EDU made efforts to combat the expanded activity of S.I. in the area of Asia and the Pacific Ocean.

On June 16th to 18th, 1983 the first convention of the Council of DUPO took place in Honolulu.

Together with the Liberal Party of Australia also participating in the convention were representatives of the conservative parties of the U.S., Canada, Japan, New Zealand and of E.D.U. One of the basic matters of the convention's agenda was how to combat Socialdemocratic ideology's influence on the area.

The great interest shown in the confrontation between EDU and the positions of Socialdemocracy can be found in the direct contacts of EDU leaders with the Americans. On August 1981 the General Secretary of EDU, Kohl, made an unofficial visit to the U.S. in order to talk with the State Department and Democratic and Republican party' officials regarding the future activity of EDU.

In the middle of February, 1982, talks had taken place in Munich between EDU leaders and representatives of the US parties referred to previously. Americans declared that lately S.I. 'causes annoyance' to Washington's leaders with its activity which is mostly directed towards disarmament and the decrease of tension. These Americans also directed EDU to reach a position of 'open confrontation' with S.I., urging EDU to start a wide propaganda programme with the purpose of 'revealing some peripheral policy of the Socialdemocrats which doesn't promote the benefits of the West'.

In the summer of 1982, in Paris, a meeting of EDU took place, which was attended by Richard Allan, a former assistant to the U.S. President on matters of National Security. He contributed a lot personally to the meeting which approved a report of an EDU subcommittee which referred to disarmament and security as seen from the American point of view. Allan had every reason to be satisfied with the results of the meeting because in that meeting some policies of the U.S. were approved such as the 'penalties' of the U.S. against USSR and also the policy of the U.S. in Latin America. In the beginning of 1983 the American administration was to the fore in the creation of the International Democratic Union (IDU) which they believed should include EDU, DUPO and the conservative parties of the U.S. and Canada with the potential also to include the Latin American section of IDU.

According to the Americans, IDU's duty was to make more coordinated efforts against S.I., to increase its productivity assisted by the U.S. both with a significant escalation of economic aid and through propaganda.

The leadership of the Republican party and Reagan personally were looking forward to the creation of IDU. As Mock said to close friends, IDU will appear to try to restore contacts and promote cooperation with SI during the solution of perplexing peripheral matters in order to weaken the influence of socialist countries and to form a protective barrier against the expansion of communist ideology. According to Mock's words some representatives of EDU and S.I. have already determined the most likely areas for their mutual activity. This concerns above all the explosively dangerous situations in Latin America and Turkey. It is proposed also to exchange views and hold organised talks on other subjects, as for example the environment and the peace movment. In a confidential discussion when the General Secretary of EDU was present together with Mock's assistant and the director of the Academy of Political Sciences, ANP, Kohl said that Mock himself had an ongoing correspondence with the president of S.I., Brandt, something which had been decided upon in the Paris convention of

EDU. According to Kohl's story, Brandt is under pressure from a dissatisfied right wing of S.I., which includes French, Italians, Spaniards and Portugese. At the same time Brandt is under pressure from the right wing of the German Socialdemocratic Party, specifically from Viznerski, with the purpose of forcing him to change the political line of the Socialdemocrats against the Nicaraguan establishment.

Reagan's Administration tries more and more to utilise the potential of the conservative forces of Western Europe. Towards this end a Centre was created in Washington regarding matters of International Relations (CIR), which under the order of the government and with their financial support publicises American Policy in West Europe and assists in the establishment of understanding, the mutual exchange of information and the promotion of co-operation between West European Countries and the U.S.A. At the beginning of March, 1983 the Centre of International relations (CIR) held, in Rome, the first convention of high level representatives of conservative scientists employed by the research institutions of U.S.A. and a series of West European countries. Representatives of Antenauer Institutions (Christian Democratic Union) and Hans Zeidel (Christian Social Union), were present.

On June 24 and 25, 1983 the Founding convention of IDU, was held in London in which were examined the foundation's problems caused by the new international organisation of conservative and Christian democratic parties. Among the founders of this global alliance was Vice-President of U.S.G. Bush. With regard to his contacts with S.I., president of IDU, Mock declared plainly that such contacts could be improved by a change of S.I.'s leadership. He also implies that IDU considers as 'positive' their ability to replace Brandt in S.I. (Vienna, 'Courier' newspaper, June 15, 1983). 'Times' of London on June 25, 1983 asserted that 'The foundation of IDU essentially constitutes an answer by right wing forces towards S.I.'s activity on the international scene.

So the right wing forces, with the Reagan administration leading, had coordinated their efforts for a new and stronger battle against the increase of Socialdemocratic ideas all around the world. S.I.'s duty though is to defend its ground against these opposition forces.

The Federation of West Germany:
The Undeclared War against Socialdemocracy

For the sovereign capitalist oligarchy of the U.S. the European Socialist movement always constituted an enemy, which was threatening to widen its ideological influence, expanding into the American continent and undermining on U.S.A.'s own ground the complete sovereignty of the economic system which is based on privacy and individuality, with the domination of the colossal industrial monopolies. The basic source of overseas 'socialist infection' after the soviet model of communism (which did not find any followers in the U.S.) is reasonably considered to be Germany, where not only was Marxism born in the middle of the 19th century, but also the most massive and well organised Social democratic party in history was founded, which later was changed by the most powerful political leaders of the country.

The first clash between American and German Socialdemocrats occured in 1945 after the collapse of Hitler's Germany, when the occupation forces of the U.S. were busy with the restoration of the state's structure in the western part of the country. Although the leaders of the West German Social democracy willingly offered to help the Americans with a view to the restoration of democracy in the country, their mutual relations with Washington never took the form of unconditional obedience.

The first President of the German Socialdemocratic Party after the war was Curt Summaher, who was a patriot and actively resisted the American plans to cut Germany into two halves, thus creating a separate West German country and converting it into a bastion of the imperialist policy of the U.S. in the European continent. Summaher and his associates in the leadership of the German Social democratic party supported the theory of Scientific Socialism, including the reduction of the omnipotence of big capital in West Germany, they also supported the idea of the nationalisation of the executive branch of industry and the widening of syndicates rights over the contractors. These theories were basic to the party's organisations. Naturally none of these were approved by Washington, which was a permanent source of conflicts and controversy.

After Summaher's death in the beginning of the '50's Socialdemocrats organised a massive campaign against the remilitarisation of West Germany and Bundesfer creation where the slogan was heard: 'Without us'. Within the German Socialdemocratic Party (GSDP) in those days the support for Germany's unification was widely held. The practical way to unify the two German countries, the Federation of West Germany (FWG) and the People's Republic of Germany (PRG) was on the bases of neutrality and their non participation in any military coalitions. With Addenauer in government the official opposition, the Socialdemocratic Party, in 1955 strongly opposed the joining of FWG in NATO. Their group in the Bundenstang, to which Brandt, Smitt and many other leaders later on belonged, unanimously voted against this fatal step which approved

Germany's division, and made the present day division of Europe into two hostile coalitions, unavoidable. Later on when the joining of West Germany in NATO was an accomplished fact, GSDP started to support the Western military alliance. This reorientation of its previous political line, was done with the approval of the Party's program of Gottsberg, in 1959.

Even that, though, did not quiet the fears of Americans concerning the loyalty of Socialdemocrats towards the pro-American governments of Bonn, which had at the top the right wing conservative forces of the Christiandemocratic Union and the Christian Socialist Union. The hostile attitude of Americans towards the German Socialdemocratic Party was quite open as long as Republicans were in the White House. In Washington it was always implied that the leaders of the Christiandemocratic Union and the Christiansocial Union made 'more acceptable partners' of the U.S. than the Socialdemocrats.

The U.S. Government was greatly concerned because West German Socialdemocrats began to advance themselves more and more at an international level and also cooperate with those of a similar persuasion in other Western European Countries. Specifically GSDP, together with Austrian and Scandinavian Socialists, was the chief worker for the revival of S.I. on a new ideological and organisational platform. With the existing 'Ebert Foundation' GSDP started to support financially the biggest part of the work for the new founded international operation. It was not a coincidence that the First Convention of S.I. in June 1951 took place in the West German city of Frankfurt, in Mein.

The founding declaration of S.I. in which the basic directions of its future activity was formulated, showed clearly to Washington that in International matters this new strong power must be considered as it would not always support the global intentions or the imperialist policy of th U.S. The ideas for democratic socialism, humanism, Social Justice and disarmament, which proceeded from S.I. largely by the initiative of GSDP, obviously did not fit in with Washington's program for the restoration and rein-forcement of American political and military leadership in the rest of the world.

American imperialists feared more than anything that because of their nature as a labour orientated party S.I.'s parties would find some forms of cooperation with the communists, or with their close friends, acceptable. Up to a degree these fears also concerned the German Socialdemocrats. At the end of the '60's in Washington, top secret evidence arrived that rep-resentatives of the left wing of GSDP were having contacts with Italian communists. Taking advantage of this opportunity the State Department of the U.S. sent a special message in 1968, to the embassy of the Federation of West Germany in Washington. The coalition government of Bonn made clear that even if Egon Bahr and Egon Franke or any other socialdemocrat reporter made contact with communists, these contacts were only for the purpose of gaining information and had nothing to do with any co-operation. This explanation though did not ease the tension and eliminate the suspicions of the Americans towards GSDP.

About the end of the '60's in the right wing press of West Germany there systematically started to appear foreign motivated reports that the Minister of Exterior, then, Willy Brandt and other members of the main office, Wenner and Bahr, and other executives of the Socialdemocratic Party were secret communists. From the style and form of these reports it became clear that behind all this was the CIA. It is of course not necessary to say that the political leadership of the USA and specifically the National Security of Washington gave the green light for all of these reports.

The gap that was separating West German Socialdemocrats and Washington became wider, when GSDP leaders, with Willy Brandt as Chief, presented a program for 'the new East policy', which was intended to make smoother the mutual relations between West Germany and the U.S.S.R. and other socialist countries of Eastern Europe, on the basis of recognition of inviolable post war borderlines, the dismissal of any claims against lands in the Eastern block and the development of mutually beneficial economic, cultural and scientific relations between the two countries.

Because of this 'new East policy', GSDP won the 1969 elections for Bundenstag and they formed the government of Social-liberal Coalition together with the Liberal Democratic Party.

One of the biggest moves of the new government was the Moscow Agreement, signed on August 12th 1970, which contained the basic principles of the 'new East policy' or GSDP. In reality, this was the first initiative by a West German government which was carried out without pre-agreement with American allies and caused concern in Washington. The American propagandists, using as their instrument the Christiandemocrat and Christian Social Union controlled media of West Germany, launched an unbridled slanderous campaign against Brandt and his followers in the leadership of GSDP. The leaders of GSDP were accused of 'secret conspiracy' with Moscow, of 'retreat from the coordinated line of West' of 'treason against the nation' etc. In the U.S. and the West-European countries of NATO rumours against Brandt started to expand; and also 'Brandt is not acceptable in the U.S.'. This was written on April 9, 1970 in the 'Washington Post' Newspaper.

A characteristic example of this slanderous campaign was the publication of the so-called Barr's documents', where in a very distorted style was reported Egon Barr's secret negotiations with Moscow which purported to show the 'treason' of Brandt towards the West. When this political scandal errupted, it was explained in the liberal and socialdemocratic Press of W. Germany that this campaign was just a method of confrontation against S.I. in co-operation with Christiandemocratic and Christian Social Union and orchestrated by Alex Springer newspapers, who was known for his close relations with West German and American 'Ultras'. It was notable that all these slanderous aspersions were immediately published in the right-wing American publications, which were often used by the CIA to disseminate scandalous propoganda.

The Campaign to Undermine Brandt and Schmitt

The easing of relations between W. Germany and U.S.S.R. and later other socialist countries of East Europe, marked the start of a period of decreasing tension, which was, during the '70's the main target in Europe. In this process the Americans were unwillingly forced to co-operate, choosing between that or international isolation. Against this background the successful Pan-European meeting for matters of security and co-operation became possible, which resulted in the approval of the Final Act of Helsinki; a real charter for peaceful co-existence between East and West. The West German Social-democrats made a significant contribution towards the establishment of a policy for the decrease of tension as the only alternative solution to a nuclear disaster. For his great personal involvement in the settling of the inter-national situation Brandt was nominated for the Nobel Prize.

The great independence which W. Germany acquired as a result of the 'East policy's' opening, caused the Americans even more concern, because Bonn's policy readily gained increasing support, both at home and among other countries of Western Europe. As a result of this, between Washington and Bonn (which was until then the most faithful U.S. ally in Europe) serious disagreements started to appear. Of course, Americans attempted to blame Socialdemocrats for that.

As soon as Americans realised that West Germany, under Social-democratic leadership and, especially, Brandt's strong political image, could go even further in its policy towards the East and could abandon the course of American-NATO policy, they decided to eliminate Brandt and his closest associates. For this purpose they sought cooperation from his political opponents of the GSDP, from the right-wing political camp. So in 1974 erupted the big political scandal of Gunther Guillaume, (personal advisor of Brandt), who was accused of 'secret contacts' with an espionage agency of the People's Republic of Germany. That case ended with the statement that Brandt knowingly was shielding Guillaume and was maintaining a 'nest of eastern spies'. Brandt was forced to resign as Chancellor but remained president of the GSDP.

However, their purpose was to finish Brandt so they organised another campaign against him, this time from the U.S.A. In 1974 the American Press and news agencies around the world spread the rumour that Brandt, prior to his career as a socialdemocrat, was a paid agent of American intelligence. Similar revelations were made by the former CIA associate, Victor Marchetti, who maintained his connections with his old bosses. The propaganda agencies of Washington tried to have exclusive rights to his story and published comments which were unfavourable to Brandt.

However Brandt's reputation was sufficiently established that these devices couldn't do him any harm. In 1975 Willy Brandt was elected President of S.I. Later on he became head of the International Committee concerning the problems of North-South relations whose leader was previously Robert McNamara the former Minister of Defence in the Kennedy and Johnson administrations, (later a director of the International Bank).

In Washington they were hoping that Helmut Schmitt who had replaced Brandt in the position of Chancellor and was known as a realist rather than an ideologist, would be more cooperative towards the American partners. Schmitt, indeed, did a lot to minimise the gap between Bonn and Washington, but Schmitt, as a Socialdemocrat, had already earned the mistrust of Washington. Although Nixon and Ford maintained some diplomatic relations with Schmitt and other German Socialdemocrat politicians, after Carter became president of the U.S. the open confrontation between Washington and Bonn became more obvious.

A prime concern of West Germany was for a decrease in world tension, something to which Washington was opposed, so German-American relations became very difficult. It was not approved that Schmitt in 1978 took the initiative in claiming that the installation in Western Europe of the new American middle range missiles was a necessity, because the Soviet Union had a superiority in this type of weapon. However Schmitt's certainty that the U.S.S.R. had superiority in missile power, was based on American statistical data which had been forged by the CIA.

After he began his initiative Schmitt, as later became plain, was caught in an American trap. Political and military leaders in Washington quietly distorted the basic idea on which was based Schmitt's claim. Schmitt, as he later explained, had started the missile talks in order to force the U.S. and U.S.S.R. to start negotiations on all matters related to middle range nuclear weapons in Europe (which pose a potentially disastrous hazzard to the European people). According to Schmitt's plan it was hoped that the two sides would prefer instead of the installation of new missiles, to negotiate for a reduction in nuclear armament and middle range missiles. Although Schmitt managed, as a result of persistent efforts, to include this point in the negotiations of the 'double solution' of NATO, after December 12, 1979, Washington completely reneged on this term and continued with the installation of the missiles anyway, while the negotiatons which started in Geneva with U.S.S.R. on this subject were doomed to be a failure from the very beginning.

This ill-omened prospect of the development of PERSHING and other missiles in West Germany revealed the growing disagreement between Washington and the W. German Socialdemocrats on matters of peace and war. The increasing confrontation between GSDP and the openly-militaristic policy of the U.S. which stemmed from Carter, gave an opportunity to Washington to make every effort to remove Socialdemocrats from the government.

In close cooperation with the right-wing leaders of both the Christian-democratic and the Christiansocial Union they began propaganda attacks against the GSDP.

Their purpose was to exploit the bad economic situation of West Germany and the mistakes made by the Social-liberal Coalition government in internal policy, as much as the disagreements between the GSDP and the Liberal Democrats in order to slander the Socialdemocrats who in losing people's support would increase the power of the Christian democrats and Christian Social Union who were led by Washington's friends, Strauss and Kohl. On the eve of elections for Budenstag which were held in 1980, in the right wing press of Western Germany a real witch hunt against the Socialdemocrats was organised with American blessing. Socialdemocrats were said to be under the influence of their left radical wing and to have formed an alliance with the communists, ready to 'stab the West in the back'. The furious attacks against Socialdemocrats followed one after the other and they were aimed not only at the left-wing but also the middle of the road leaders of GSDP to persuade them to believe Brandt's connections with CIA and also Soviet espionage. All these events occurred after Carter's official

85

declaration (which was made at Brandt's personal request) which pronounced all these suspicions to be 'absolutely groundless' especially condemning what the Washington Post had written about Brandt. The former correspondent of 'The New York Times' in Bonn, David Beynter, wrote that: 'I get the shivers from the dirty war of slander waged against this respectable man'.

In the elections of 1980, Socialdemocrats as a whole managed to maintain their position and to re-form, together with the Liberal Democrats, the coalition government.

Right after that though, Ronald Reagan came to power in Washington with his ultra-conservative administration which seems to have a natural allergy to any relationship with Socialism. Right from the beginning it became clear that Reagan would not seek to find any common ground for discussion, even with such a moderate Socialdemocrat as Helmut Schmitt. The relations between the USA and Socialdemocratic W. Germany soon reached a state of crisis.

In Washington they could not understand why Schmitt refused to join the 'crusade' against the USSR which was started with Reagan at the head soon after his entrance to the White House. Bonn's chancellor gave warning that every kind of effort to retreat from the policy of (ΥΦΕΣΗΣ) and revive the cold war between East and West in order to bring pressure against Moscow by the approval of enormous military programs and an escalation in the arms race with the intention of achieving a military superiority against USSR, was doomed to failure and also included the danger of a nuclear war explosion in which no one could claim to be the winner.

Schmitt and the Socialdemocrat leaders who supported him in Bonn's government, pointed out that W. Germany and the other Western European countries were greatly concerned about Washington's theories regarding a limited nuclear war against USSR which would occur only on European ground and would undoubtedly destroy the whole European civilisation, without impinging upon the USA. The first victims of this nuclear disaster would be the Germans, as even the Americans confess.

Having in mind W. Germany's sad experience regarding the unsuccessful boycott of the Moscow Olympic Games in 1980, Schmitt's administration did not intend to follow Washington's latest political line, when by exploiting the incidents in Afghanistan and Poland, they tried to isolate the USSR internationally, to postpone Madrid's meeting and to impose an economic boycott against the USSR with an embargo and annulment of the undersigned agreements which were of more interest to the Western countries than the Soviet.

Bonn also refused to support Reagan's policy of expansion in the third world countries, which would result in an artificial increase of tension and the creation of centres of military conflict in the Middle East, Africa and Central America. Simultaniously Schmitt and the members of his government repeatedly demonstrated that the way Reagan's administration treated the allies and the complete disregard of their lawful rights, were unacceptable. More specifically, with their high interest rates policy, Washington tried to face (not to the benefit of Europe) their own economic difficulties in the U.S. and to cover the inflated deficit in the U.S.A. balance of payments which was a result of huge military expenses. For Europeans this resulted in the export of capital from Europe, a decrease in production and an increase in inflation and unemployment.

Reagan's associates eventually came to the conclusion that the increasing opposition of Bonn created a persistent danger to the successful outcome of their capitalist policy. The answer was to overthrow the Social Liberal Coalition of W. Germany.

Everybody in Washington knew that the opposition, a coalition between Christian democratic and Christian Social Union who had lost every hope of winning the elections, intended to wreck this last coalition from the inside and attract to its side the newest partners in GSDP, the Liberal Democrats, with Vice-Chancellor and minister of the exterior, Genser, as leader. In furthering such a 'coup-de-etat at court' not only the propaganda mechanism and the special services of Washington participated but the officials also. In the inhospitable reception of Bonn's Socialdemocrats in Washington, Reagan's administration showed greater kindness towards the opposition Christiandemocrat politicians like Genser. In 1981–82 the American press wrote that the American government acted as if the Christian democrats were in power in W. Germany instead of the Social-democrats.

To demonstrate the hostile articles in the American Press against Schmitt and his Socialdemocrat associates the following incident is an example: The greatest supporter of Reagan's administration 'The New York Times' observer William Sofayer, on February of 1982, held a press conference with Bonn's Chancellor for an hour, but from the whole text which covered 20 pages, he chose only two points, which he used in his later article to demonstrate Schmitt's unacceptable policy in relation to the USA.

In the US congress Schmitt was openly accused of tolerating the existence of 'a second government' in Bonn, led by Willy Brandt, who 'works with the Kremlin for the escalation of a long term campaign organised by Moscow to spread misinformation in Germany and the whole of Europe through S.I.'

'Another congressman claimed that Social-Liberal government leads West Germany to a new 'ΑΥΤΟΦΙΝΛΑΝΑΟΠΟΙΗΣΗ)'.

As regards the strong anti-war and anti-missile movement existing in W. Germany which is steadfastly supported by GSDP, the official authorities of Washington did not consider it necessary to hide their hostility towards West German Socialdemocrats and Schmitt's government. In their public announcements American politicians and diplomats started to suggest that Bonn's policy was planned by 'neutrals and pacifists' who intended to take W. Germany out of NATO and thus would endanger the 'ability of Europe to defend itself'.

What the political spokesman of Washington left unsaid, was said in July '82 by Richard Allen, the President's assistant on matters of National security, who was also counsellor to the Republican party on international matters and a personal friend of Reagan, and who, later on, resigned. In his speech to the Conservative European Democratic Union Convention in Paris, Allen furiously attacked West German Socialdemocrats, calling Willy Brandt 'internationally dangerous' and S.I.'s policy which Brandt is planning, 'unreasonable'.

Possibly, sooner or later, the secret means which Washington used to overthrow the Social-liberal coalition of Bonn on September '82, will come to the surface. In any case it is without doubt that the Americans participated in that 'cold blooded coup-de-etat' brought about by the treason of Genser and the Liberal Democrats towards their Socialdemocrat partners. It is widely known in any case, that the right wing leaders of the Christiandemocrat and Christian Social Union led by Genser, who took power, were just the sort of material with which Washington liked to work.

It is undoubtedly true that the massive psychological pressure which Washington applied on the West European voters, together with media controlled by right wing forces in W. Germany, played an important role in the victory of the new centrist coalition of Christian democratic and Christian Social Union and the Liberal Democrats in the elections of March '83 for Bundenstag. During the campaign before the elections they stressed the slander against GSDP mainly for its 'disruptive effect' on Social-democrats that they were a leading power in S.I. concerns. The General Secretary of the Christiandemocratic Union, H. Geisler, called the Social-democrats 'gangs of criminals'. Geisler, and also the other leaders of the Christian democratic – Christian Social Union, were repeatedly accusing GSDP of 'retreating from the common principles of German and Western policies of peace and security'. Strauss' newspaper 'Bayern Courier' tried to prove that 'Socialdemocrats knowingly are trying to detach West Germany from the U.S.A. and that 'they cultivate an anti-american mood in the country'. 'The actions of GSDP leaders', Die Welt of Spieger claimed, 'are causing confusion in Europe and the U.S.'.

To that propaganda the American Press, guided by the CIA, contributed a great deal. Thus, for example, papers that closely supported Reagan commented that GSDP used S.I. as an 'obedient tool' of its 'anti-western' policy and it applied to this international organisation the label of pacifism. Also at this time efforts were made to slander the leaders of West German Socialdemocracy. Targets of these cheap inventions directed by the West German right wing and approved by the U.S.A. became not only Brandt, Schmitt, Wenner, Barr, Emke, Epiler and Lafontain but also the candidate selected from the GSDP for chancellor's position, Hans Johan Foggel. Without any reason he was accused of having an 'active nazi past'.

Immediately after the announcement of the results of the elections for Bundenstag in March, 1983, Washington applauded. 'The impressive victory of conservative parties in the West German elections was accepted with enthusiasm and relief by Reagan's administration officials', wrote 'The Washington Post' on March 7, 1983.

As 'The New York Times' wrote at that time, a State Department official concerned with matters of relationship between USA and W. Germany confessed that Washington's government 'had been seriously concerned about the possibility of a Socialdemocrat victory as they had Hans Johan Foggel as leader'. When the news of a Christiandemocratic victory became known, the same official declared: 'The west has been saved'. Another official representative declared that 'In any case, Washington will not now need to face Bonn's criticism against U.S. policy concerning relations with the USSR'.

The unrestrained slanderous propaganda against the West German Socialdemocrats and S.I. is still continuing at this present time in W. Germany and the U.S.

10

French Socialists Under the Pressure of the U.S.

The distrust of the Reagan's administration towards every socialist government reflects the traditional thinking of overseas conservatives towards socialist parties. Thus, in France, the pink colour of French Socialists appears to Americans to be deep red. Serious differences between Paris and Washington were existing on an economic level regarding the Third World (Latin America, Near and Middle East) and on trade with the East etc. In order to reduce the autonomy of the Morreir government, Washington picked on a policy of pressure and the Americans never stopped their efforts towards the destabilisation of the situation in France, in order to up-root 'the marxist conspiracy'.

Characteristic examples are given below:

1. In 1978 during the preparation of constitutional elections for the French parliament, Americans started to depend on the right wing politicians in their campaign to humiliate Mitterrand.

In January the U.S. Embassy announced the results of a meeting of Socialist leaders with Carter during his stay in Paris, indicating that this meeting was made possible only after persistent requests from Mitterrand. This of course did not correspond to the real reason for the meeting.

American's position proved to be an invention of the right wing politicians. Their story was that Mitterrand was refusing to meet with the President of France, Giscard d'Estaign; and rejected his policy. Thus it appeared that the first secretary of the Socialist Party had no faith in the political powers of France prefering to meet the U.S. President rather than talking with the president of his own country.

2. The U.S.A. tried to stabilise the position of the right wing parties in France. After the Socialist Party gained power, relations between America and the right-wing parties extended beyond accepted limits. Washington officials tried to effect a coalition of the right-wing, using as its hub the mayor of Paris, Chirac, who was called by Haig 'leader of the French opposition'; something which was not true. As an example of the special relations between Reagan and Chirac we must refer to the confidential visits to Paris of General Walters (who is one of Reagan's closest associates and a

former sub-director of CIA) when returning from his trip abroad. During his visit to the U.S. Chirac was received by Reagan personally, though prior to that the leaders of French opposition parties never met with Reagan.

3. The U.S.A. considered that a weakening of the economic position of Morreir government would in a great degree weaken the ability of Mitterrand's administration to manouvre a political break from the Philo-American political line. Not by chance, Washington took a series of measures to weaken French economic power. The American controlled press published an announcement about a possible depreciation of the Franc. This information was supposedly gained during Mitterand's talk with American reporters. In Paris the government denied this story but a state of panic was created which cost French Banks huge amounts of money spent in trying to maintain the value of the national currency.

Possibly as a result of this continous 'flow' of information the contents of a telegram which was sent by Goldbright, American Ambassador to France, became known, pointing out the pressure applied against the branches of French Banks in order to force them to take a loan from the French State. In the hard light of day, Americans could not discriminate the real truth from his purposefully distributed misinformation. Eventually French customs authorities discoverd that in the branch of the American Mortgage Bank, managed by Merryl Lynch in France, (Ronald Reagan held this position until he became Economic minister) there was an involvement in the illegal export of French currency abroad. That was part of the strategy to undermine the French economic system.

4. In May 1982 'Liberation', a Paris newspaper published the text of an article written by a diplomat at the American Embassy in Paris, named John Dobrin, who drew a political caricature of President Francois Mitterand. In this article Mitterand is scornfully portrayed as a man who thinks in 'feigned ideas and abstract purposes', and less than any other candidate who failed to be elected 'understands strategic problems'. In the story it was pointed out that Mitterand himself doesn't understand the modern problems of security and he is not 'sufficiently informed'. That article was written by the State Department ten days after Mitterand was elected President.

In the period of time immediately following the elections, U.S. officials and especially the U.S. Ambassador to France, Goldbright, made repeated suggestions and indicated directly what the policy of the new French government should be.

In connection with the U.S. and the French Socialists we noted some selections from the Press at that time:

1. Activity of the CIA in France during the post-war period:

– It helped to create Force Ouvrier Syndicate as a counter weight to the Federation of W. Germany.

– Supplied with money many distinguished followers of the idea of a United Europe, also funded the Socialists.

– Indirectly participated in financial support of (ΠPIOB) magazine, and (ΛIO ΠOΠOYΛEP) and (KOMIIA) newspapers.

– It recruited gangsters to unload American ships of supplies according to the Marshall Plan (in order to eliminate boycott).

– It tried to bribe Socialists' leader Guy Mauller, offering him 75,000 dollars to thwart General de Gaulle's ambitions for power. (Guy Mauller supported the General and CIA's money disappeared).

(Monde Diplomatique, February of 1975).

1. In 1977 Fred Hearse' and Richard Flencher's brochure, 'CIA and the labour movement' which was published in London, revealed details of financial aid given to the United Europe Movement by the CIA after the war. In that brochure it was explained that 'CIA organised a system which brought together British Labour Party members, people who were involved with the application of the Marshall Plan and the Bildberg group for their mutual benefit. This whole system concealed from publicity has never been disbanded with the result that we find people devoted to the American cause in important positions in Western Europe at this present time.

(Monde Diplomatique, February of 1978)

3. In May 1977, the American issue of Business week Magazine simultaneously with the right-wing French Minute published rumours about Mitterand's deadly illness. 'Supposing (the same newspaper wrote in the middle of the pre-election battle in France) that Mitterand suffers seriously from Hodgkins disease which appears to effect the lymphatic glands with swelling and inflamation, we doubt if he could participate actively in the pre-election campaign for the National Assembly... without this famous french leader, the possibilities of a left wing coalition came to nothing'.

(Monde, May 21, 1977)

From Giscard d'Estaign's quarters the rumours about Mitterand supposedly suffering from cancer continue to be spread.

(Canar Ansene June 8, 1983)

4. In the years 1975–1976 Americans were applying pressure on French

92

politicians to give up any connection with communists. Thus, for example, when Mitterand met Kissinger in Washington in November 1975, Kissinger warned him that 'the European cemeteries are full of politicians who thought that they could manage communists'. After that meeting 'Kissinger's doubts on the basic issue of whether or not the French government could stay in the NATO alliance while having communists in their administration, could not be dissolved'-

(Tass, May 15, 1981, and Monde, Nov. 27, 1975)

On February 22, 1976 General Haig declared: 'The most serious problem which NATO faces at the present time is the participation of Marxists in Western governments'. AFP news agency gave a different interpretation to these reports: 'In other countries of West Europe (except Portugal) the participation of marxist parties in the administration is unacceptable to me'.

(Monde, Febr. 24, 1976)

'The American Ambassador in Paris, Kenneth Rass, welcoming in March 1976 Mitterand's assistants, Claude Estée and Gill Martiné, declared that the U.S. would not tolerate the participation of Communists in any other French government'.

(Monde, March 3, 1976)

Commenting on the last of the meetings between Carter and the French leaders in Paris, two months before the parliamentary elections of 1978, Cotidien dio Paris newspaper wrote that the 'U.S.A. are trying to revive the great pro-american coalition of Mitterand-Rober Fabre-Jan Lecanue'(that means the left of Centre but without the Communists as had previously been tried in Italy).

(Tass, January 9, 1978)

5. The victory of the left wing in France on May 10th, 1981 caused Washington concern because, according to Le Monde newspaper, May 12, 1981 'Americans in the highest positions are very sensitive to red, while the world 'Socialism' affects Reagan's nerves'. Washington immediately sent to Paris the notice that 'to the U.S. of course it makes a difference what is going to be the formation of the French government'.

(Matin, May 13, 1981)

That was affirmed officially by the State Department's representative D. Fisher: 'The administration carefully observes the political process in

France and, especially, expresses its interest in the formation of the new government'.

(Tass, June 5, 1981)
Congressman Josef Byden warned: 'I believe sincerely that Mitterand must not compromise with the French Communist Party in order to form a government. This could cause damage'.

(Matin, May 13, 1981)
On the same day the New York Times wrote: 'American governments as a general rule resent the participation of Communists in the governments of any country with which they are allied, even in the most insignificant positions, because Washington fears that maybe this would cause a weakening of the alliance and hamper measures taken to achieve a neutral Europe'.

After the formation of the leftist government in France, Washington made an official declaration: 'The participation of Communists in this government or any other government of our West European allies will seriously affect our relationship with them'.

(Washington Post, June 26, 1981)
Wall Street Journal pointed out: 'Mitterand' destroyed one of the pillars which supports the Atlantic community – the principle of resistance against any sharing of power with the Communists'.

(Monde, July 5–6, 1981)
In May–June 1981 the Americans, trying to influence Mitterand in various ways, made it clear that in case of any participation by Communists in the French Government they would:
– Endanger the supply to France of American intelligence information in Europe and the Persian Gulf.
– Cause the Arab countries, especially Saudi Arabia, to reach the obvious conclusions from this 'American provision' and they would not therefore deposit money in French Banks.
– Cause the French example to be reflected in Greece, Spain and Italy which would lead to the weakening of NATO.

Maybe the American right wing were responsible for the publishing of a red-painted geographical map of France with the slogan: 'Save Spain, France is already fallen'.

6. The appointment of the known leftist extremist (one of Che Guevarra's followers) Razie Debre was a blow to the Americans. On this subject many different political opinions were heard. The most curious ones are the following:

– The American magazine 'Business Week' on November 2, 1981 wrote: 'It is surmised that Razie Debre's influence over Mitterand has something to do with the talk we very often hear about the close friendship between Debre and Mitterands wife. 'Americans say that after Debre's appointment, Fidel Castro appointed Alfredo Guevarra as Cuba's representative to UNESCO in Paris. Alfredo Guevarra is a personal friend of Debre and a confident of Castro. He is known to western agents as an associate of the Cuban secret services. Washington believes that through Debre and Guevarra, Mitterand will contact Fidel Castro'.

7. American authorities apply strong pressure on French Socialist leaders in order to change the favourable attitude of Paris towards Latin America and some other countries, establishments, national movements or leaders (eg Castro) which the U.S. consider to be dangerous.

As a result of such pressure, the meeting of Socialist International office which was to take place in Caracas on February 25 1982, was postponed.

8. 'The new forces in Western European Socialdemocracy (especially the youth) started actively to confront the two historical taboo's which for many years was an agreement with the capitalist way of development and a strategic solidarity with Washington. These expressions grew as a result of the Euro-leftist movement. After they granted positions to the Communist Parties, which are not related in their politicasl views with soviet Foreign policy, Euro-leftists who are still only in the early stages could help Europe achieve political autonomy, on the understanding though that a new concept in their relations with the Third World, instead of the old one, (which endeavours to spread capitalism internationally), would be developed'.

9. After the Williamsburg meeting, in spite of Mitterand's 'atlantic

obedience', Shultz expressed his indignation towards the French government, with whom 'the solution of problems concerning the allies becomes more and more difficult'. One of Shultz's assistants explained 'We understand that Mitterand needs to stay at a distance from the West countries alliances for political reasons but it doesn't mean that we approve'.

(New York Times 6/12/83 – Tass 6/13/83)

10. In a comment about the transatlantic differences in the respected Swiss newspaper, Journal Dio Jeneff, the philo-American intentions of Mitterand were vigorously criticised. 'The French government has for three years now worked with false presuppositions. It hopes that by being the best student in the Atlantic school and providing Reagan with proofs of its anti-soviet feelings, it could receive from Washington more help for the economic problems that the French Socialist government faces. In reality the undoubted surrender of France to Washington, not only reduces France's freedom of manouvre in its foreign policy, but also contradicts the French and W. Germany policy which was followed by Giscard d'Estaign and Schmidt and which had the effect of making these two countries, and the whole of Europe, much more independent of the U.S.A. than now.

(Journal Dio Zeneff, April 28, 1983)

11
The U.S.A. and the British Labour Party

At the Labour Party's conference in Blackpool in 1981, it was stated that the establishment and protection of peace around the world had first priority. The conference made an appeal for the immediate start of negotiations regarding the problem of the installation of American missiles in Great Britain. The Labour Party declared their dedication to the idea of creating a missile free zone in Europe, and their resentment against the NATO or Warsaw Agreement. The conference made an appeal for all members of the party to actively support, inside and outside the country, the main campaign for disarmament, with the purpose of implementing the proposals which had been made by the special synod of the U.N.'s general assembly on disarmament in 1978. In the report of S.I.'s work team in 1981, the position of the British Labour Party was stated which had been made clear in the declaration of the Labour parties conference, suggesting the prohibition of any nuclear bases (British or American) on British ground or in British territorial waters. Such an attitude of the Labour Party, which basically was reaffirmed at the Party's conference in 1983, would, of course, cause Washington much displeasure.

The U.S.A. were especially concerned about the left wing of the Labour Party, which had since the Bevan era supported the spread of Socialist ideas and criticised vigorously the efforts to replace Socialism by State Capitalism as the right wing of the party wanted. The right wing, in fact were actually controlling the political line of the party until the split.

The left wing of the labour party holds political views publicised by 'The Tribune' newspaper (an earlier editor of which was Michael Foot) which, following a tradition, did not hesitate to criticise vigorously the foreign policy of the American administration, especially during the Vietnam war. In the middle of the '60's the position of the left wing became stronger because of a change in the balance of power, especially after trade unions gained strength, (by the syndicate of skilled and unskilled transport workers, and the syndicate of machinists) the left wing members of the party demanded that their right wing labour leadership, and also the government, should quit their philo-american policy.

The reinforcement of the role of left wing members inside the party and the increasing confrontation between left wing groups and the executive committee of the Labour Party on one hand and the Members of Parliament controlled by right wing Labourites on the other, caused the Americans to fear that the whole Labour Party could veer towards left wing political views and become a source of anti-American feeling in England.

The Americans fear (not without reason) some anti-U.S. policy which a possible Labour government could produce, because, according to them, the party has veered too much toward the left wing. That is why Reagan's administration came to the conclusion that it must thwart the Labour Party's ambition to regain government. Brewster, the U.S. Ambassador to England, said confidentially, that the basic method by which the Americans intended to shake the Labour Party's position was by widening the differences inside the Party.

Brewster also said that Americans are more in favour of escalation of right wing activity. the right wing aims to split the Party and to create a new Socialdemocratic Political organisation. At the same time, using their connection with the British Press, the American's began a propaganda campaign aimed at undermining the confidence of Labour Party's voters. They were mainly behind the wide media campaign which suggested that Trotskyists, Maoists and Communists had penetrated the ranks of the Labour Party.

The State Department was continuously giving orders to the American Embassy in London to maintain closer contacts with those distinguished Labour Party members who could influence Party policy. The Americans were taking care not only to maintain their ties with right wing representatives, but also to restore a semi-official relationship with distinguished left wing members of the Party. As Brewster states 'the Embassy maintains cordial and friendly relations' with one of the leaders of the left wing, called Heffer, (a member of the national executive committee of the Party). The Americans restored 'good and fertile relations' with other reputable members of the left wing of the Labour Party, as, for example, Cook, Fenner Brockway and so on. Taking into consideration that the Labour Party is greatly influenced by the unions, the U.S. Embassy took great care to restore and maintain close contacts with the leaders of the bigger trade–unions.

Regarding Foot to be a transitory political figure in the position of Party's leaders, the Americans took steps to make prior contact with his possible successor.

They also, while maintaining the close relations formed with the leaders of the right wing such as Healey, Mason and Hattersley, paid a lot of attention to the representatives of the centre, particularly to Shore and Silkin.

Referring to the results of this policy, Brewster was able to point out that 'the Americans for the moment have many trusted friends inside the Labour Party leadership, who will be glad to help in an emergency situation'.

The impetus towards a split in the Party which was created by the apearance of 'The Gang of Four' (R. Jenkins, D. Owen, W. Rogers, S. Williams), was a source of relief to the American government. All the members of 'the gang of four' were distinguished for their tough philo-NATO and philo-American ideas which did not clash with their socialist ideas. However, the Americans were concerned that 'the gang of four' did not have any social base and if it departed from the Party's ranks without the support of the unions, it would not be able to play a very important role in England's political life.

At the beginning, Americans thought that the existence of the 'gang of four' inside the party would impose more restraint on M. Foot and his followers than their departure from the Party, and that the right wing Labourites would succeed in gaining control of the Party's leadership. As it happened though, the Labour Party election manifesto contained many foreign policy statements which actually would discredit the American overseas policy in Europe, and forced them to reform their tactics.

CIA immediately began a programme to widen the split in the Labour Party, and started to support, both morally and materially, the chief participants in the split. The logic of these activities was simple. In reality the new party of Socialdemocrats, even in an alliance with the Liberals, had a minimum chance of success. Because of the traditional balance of power between Labour and Conservative in England during the post-war years, success in the elections was usually dependent on between 1 and 3 per cent, therefore a possible split in the Labour Party caused the hopes of a Labour victory to recede.

After the split in the Labour Party the CIA turned all it's efforts towards the reorientation of Labours political line, including the detachment of Foot and his followers from the leadership and the reinforcement of Healey's group which had been distinguished for its pro-American feelings for a long time. The 'danger' that Labour was likely to gain power had passed, but the Labour Party, with its policy of rejection of American missiles and favour of unilateral disarmament, still constituted an important power in reinforcing the movement against war in Europe.

12

North European Countries Under American Fire

In 1981 amongst those regarded unfavourably by the White House was the Norwegian Labour Party (NLP). The force of American criticism was turned against Norwegian Prime Minister Gru harlem Brundlandt, personally. The reason for this was that Brundlandt and her Party favoured the creation of a missile free zone in North Europe. This caused fears in the U.S. that if in the autumn of '81 Brundlandt should win the elections, the talks for a missile free zone would be repeated in Norway. Reagan's administration was quite open in its concern about these talks, which could lead to more and more extensive neutral zones in Western Europe. In order to reduce the possibilities of Brundlandt gaining victory, the American newspapers started to condemn her for her intention 'to weaken the defence of the Atlantic Alliance'.

When the NLP was in opposition, Brundlandt made efforts to expand the idea of a missile free zone in the northern party of Europe: something which contributed to the escalation of the anti-war movement in Norway.

On February 9, 1982, by an anonymous phone call, Brundlandt was threatened that during her speech one of the local organisations of NLP would be attacked. The responsibility for the attack was claimed by the terrorist neo-nazi organisation 'Norwegian German Army', which had connections with the CIA.

On February 1983, in her speech to members of the national leadership of NLP, Brundlandt accused Reagan of not making any effort to transact serious negotiations in Geneva. She said that the Reagan inspired policy was the cause of increasing distrust between the U.S.A. and West Europe.

In response to this accusation the American Embassy in Oslo declared that Brundlandt's speech 'not only hurt the U.S. President personally but damaged the security of every NATO member'. In a comment about the American government's action the Norwegian newspaper, Arbiderblander, wrote that 'Washington had regarded the Norwegian Labour Party with disapproval for a long time'.

During the visit of Vice-President Bush to Norway in July 1983, he tried to apply pressure on NLP's leaders to dissuade them from possible attempts to 'weaken the common position of the NATO countries through the projection of different initiatives on matters of disarmament. The American Vice-President also tried to prove that the U.S. more than any other country, provided aid to Nicaragua, and called on the leaders of NLP to support the leader of the so-called 'Revolutionary Front of Santino' E. Pastore who, according to Bush, was an acceptable political figure to the U.S.A.'.

The U.S.A. versus Danish Socialists

In 1980, through the agency of pro-american western reporters, a new word was added to the vocabulary of commentators: 'Danisation' which gained meaning through the fact that the Danish government would not agree to the total figure which was predestined to be spent on the general military preparations of the West.

Later on the American newspapers were responsible for a suspicious 'leak', CIA's way of publishing the contents of top secret letters from former U.S. Defence Minister Brown to the Danish Government. Their publication was meant to create the impression that Jorgensen's government had so weakened Denmark's defences that the country could not withstand a possible Russian attack until the NATO forces could come to their rescue.

In the beginning of 1981, American propaganda attacks against Jorgensen increased even more. Jorgensen himself was called 'propagandist of zero choice' in Europe where it was expected that the maintenance of military expenses could be kept at today's figures ('zero increase'). They started to call Jorgensen 'Salvator Alliente of Denmark', and his policy on defence and security 'political illusions', which are as far from reality as the psychedelic delusions of people who use LSD'. What to the U.S. were delusions, were, for Jorgensen an objective estimation of the situation around the world and especially in North Europe. He made it clear at a press conference with Danish reporters, after a meeting of the office of Socialist International in Bonn in the summer of 1981, that he was not following the same path as the White House. During this discussion, Jorgensen supported the widening of the missile free zone, not only in the north but also in other areas of Europe, pointing out that even if Americans reject the idea of a missile free zone it doesn't necessarily mean that this idea is dead.

In April 1981 in the House of Representatives of the American Congress it was inferred (on the matter of the armed forces) that while Denmark was sheltered under NATO's umbrella, it did not want to pay for such protection. It was suggested that Denmark should spend more money on defence and less on social services.

Expressing the official view in Washington of such disobedient allies as Denmark, the Democrat Senator from Delaware, G. Byden, said that the Americans would eventually have to find a way to teach responsibility to every country-member of NATO which spends less money than the others on military expenses.

Commenting about the attacks of Washington against Jorgensen and his administration, in May 1981, the Associated Press characterised them as a verbal campaign for the defamation of Denmark as partners of the U.S. in NATO.

A short time before Jorgensen's resignation, Washington showed once again its displeasure against the Danish Prime Minister and his administration with regard to international matters. Jorgensen did not receive an invitation to visit the U.S.A. for the traditional reception of a country's leader, who rightfully occupies the position of president of the Committee of the European Council in Brussels.

During his speech in June, 1983, Nilsen the supervisor of the Press Department in the Danish Foreign Affairs ministry, declared that the mutual good relations between the USA and Denmark are absolutely natural during a conservative administration, bearing in mind Reagan's hatred towards Danish socialdemocrats and their leader Jorgensen. The Americans express complete sympathy for the difficulties of Sleutter's government and they promise him every kind of aid.

Thus, for example, trying to avoid discussion in parliament, which could disrupt the new government, on the matter of Denmarks contribution towards fulfilling NATO's plans regarding the installation of middle range American missiles in West Europe, America suggested that Sleutter retreat. In meetings with members of the Danish government, the American correspondents in Copenhagen inferred that the reduction of the Danish contribution to the Euro-missiles installation posed only an insignificant problem which from the material point of view can easily be covered by the U.S.A.

Traces of the CIA in Sweden also.

The way in which the CIA acts in order to 'neutralise' the policies of Socialdemocrat leaders and their governments unfavourable to the White House is obvious in the example of the unforgettable Swedish Prime Minister, Olaf Palme. His surveillance by the CIA shows that U.S. espionage recruits people who have direct contact with the Socialdemocrats who are on their list. At the end of the '40's the CIA recruited an agent who during that period of time had studied with Palme at Canyon College, Ohio (newspaper EXPRESSIEN, January 1983).

In the '60's when Palme was actively fighting against the Vietnam War, this agent was sent to Sweden. His duty was to 'restore contact' with Palme from whom he could extract information about any anti-American feeling inside the leadership of Swedens Socialdemocratic Party; also to collect any evidence which could be used in the future for the defamation of Palme, who was at that time Minister of Education.

This agent was working openly in front of the Swedish police and the Swedish security service, called SEPO, which for some strange reason kept silence and didn't warn Palme.

In those days the CIA considered Palme to be a 'radical personality'. At the end of the '60's the CIA suspected Palme of giving documents which slandered the U.S. president, to North Vietnam. CIA recommended that SEPO give less chance to the Swedish Police to collect secret information, something that they had been doing.

Obviously, the Americans gave 'orders' in this following case too. In the administrative circles of the Ministry of the Exterior in Sweden it is becoming recognised that the further promotion of the creation of a missile free zone in Central Europe was significantly hampered by the rightwing forces, who instigated a campaign against Palme, accusing him of making his proposal in co-operation with, and specifically at, Barr's direction. The publication in the Swedish Press of a top secret document from the Swedish Ministry of the Exterior which confirmed the existance of an agreement between Palme and Barr caused the Swedish Prime Minister much political damage. Palme was also defending himself from attacks by the conservatives, (March of 1983).

CIA had been involved in the differences between Sweden and Denmark over the problem of defining economic spheres in the Baltic Sea. During the period of the installation of their missiles in West Europe, the Americans were trying to detach Denmark from its northern partners in order to create external political difficulites for Sweden, and also for the Prime Minister Olaf Palme, who in their opinion was going 'too much to the left' regarding matters of disarmament and missile free zones.

'Conspiracy' on Danube's Banks
Also in Austria

On Washington's black list, one of the first names to appear after the W. German Socialdemocrats is the name of the Austrian Socialists. The case doesn't reach such extremes as when in the history of 'Austrian Marxism' Austria gave to the world many people who were distinguished theorists of Scientific Socialism whose themes are often reflected in the actions of the leaders of todays Austrian Socialist Party.

To the American conservatives, people like Rener Petermann and Kreisky who occupied positions in the left wing of the International Socialist Movement, were always as 'red' as Summaher, Brandt or Wener. The fact that Austrian Socialists together with West German and Scandinavian Socialdemocrats are the founders of Socialist International, while B. Petterman, the president of the Austrian Socialist Party from 1964–76, was also president of S.I. gave additional reasons for the distrust felt by official Washington.

A target of suspicion to the overseas right wing was always the experienced leader of the Austrian Socialist Party (ASP). Bruno Kreisky, who for 13 years, until April 1983, was Federal Chancellor of Austria. He became distinguished amongst the most respected West German politicians. In the eyes of the American oligarchy, Kreisky was condemned by his active anti-fascist past and his close cooperation with the (according to the Americans) 'radical' leaders of the West German and the Scandinavian Socialdemocrats, especially with Willy Brandt and Olaf Palme, with whom Kreisky had maintained contact since he was an immigrant in Sweden during the Second World War. Between these people there was not only, in most cases, completely indentical views, but also personal friendship. Not incidentally, right wing American publications when attacking S.I. always referred to the 'harmful' role of the trio: Brandt-Kreisky-Palme.

Kreisky had earned the ill disguised animosity of Washington with his decisive statements in favour of the maintenance and reinforcement of Austrian neutrality, also for Austria's active role in smoothing relations between the countries of East and West Europe and the creation of a pan European security system. Together with Brandt, Kreisky is considered to be one of the founders of *commission* policy, responsible for the decrease in international tension and the peaceful co-existence of Capitalism and Socialism. As was later made clear he couldn't satisfy the warlike-minded conservative leaders of West. He made a great personal contribution to the convocation of the Pan European Conference for Security and Cooperation and to the approval of the Final Act of the meeting in Helsinki, which placed obstacles in the way of the Reagan Administration from the position of power as it is today.

Washington also condemened Kreisky for his critical speeches which were aimed at the military policy of the U.S.A., which intends to escalate the arms race, and at the inconsiderate actions of Washington in Near and Middle East, Central America and South Africa. Obviously Reagan didn't like Kreisky's appeals which were aimed at keeping America out of Poland's internal problems, stopping the dramatisation of events in Afganistan, and stopping Third World conflicts interfering in the mutual relations between the two superpowers.

Indignation with Washington's 'falcons' was the reason for the direct contact between Kreisky and the leaders of the Palestinian Liberation Movement, especially with the leader of the Libyan Revolution, Khaddafi, whom the USA call 'the most dangerous terrorist in the world'. Kreisky's activity as head of the Special Committee of S.I. in Near East countries, had, as its purpose, the elaboration of rational alternative solutions to the non productive American policy of Camp David. It also ignited a fire.

Washington's anger at the independent policy of Austria in international matters is displayed from time to time in the intensive anti-Austrian attacks by officials in Reagan's Administration: In May, 1982 the high standing State Department official, Douglas, condemned the Austrian policy of neutrality and their maintenance of good neighbour relations with the East. These statements were immediately answered by the Austrian minister of Foreign Affairs, B. Parr, who pointed out that the interpretation of a policy of neutrality is strictly a matter for the Austrian government and that Austria had the right to completely maintain its positions in the sphere of international policy, even if these positions are different from those of the U.S.

In December 1982 another attempt was made to apply pressure on neutral Austria and the Austrian Socialist Party's government. In relation to the intensive talks at that time, regarding the American embargo on supplies of equipment required for installation of the gas pipe which was to connect Siberia – West Europe, the USA deputy minister of Defence, F. Ikley, asked Austria to reduce their mutually beneficial trade relations with U.S.S.R. threatening that unless they did economic sanctions would be imposed by the U.S.A. Ikley alleged also that Austrian policy with regard to U.S.S.R. posed a 'danger to Western security'.

The same accusations were levelled against Austria by the pro-USA government 'Business Week' magazine, which alleged that more than a hundred Austrian companies were employed in the illegal supply of western technology with strategic significance to the U.S.S.R. Kreisky, who learned about these attacks only from the newspapers, reacted immediately, declaring that Washington's government made their attacks not directly, but through the Press, which is under Washington's control.

In spite of all this, Washington's leaders continued to hide their dislike of Kreisky and his policies beneath a series of polite phrases and reasurances that between the USA and Austria 'there are not any kind of problems', during Kreisky's visit to the U.S., in February 1983, when the first meeting in person between the Austrian Chancellor and the President of the U.S. took place.

Reagan hypocritically praised Kreisky for his 'wisdom in handling problems of state'. This apparent diplomatic courtesy though did not prevent the White House and State Department, through the existing secret channels controlled by the CIA, from strengthening the systematic campaign to undermine Kreisky's position and the position of the leading Austrian Socialist Party.

In Washington they were already counting on the removal of the Socialists from power in Austria and their replacement by the Opposition Popular Party which displays pro-American feelings. For this purpose, in the Austrian conservative press and that of other West European countries, especially West Germany, comments are often published which are intended to prove the inability of the Austrian Socialist Party to govern the country ánd solve internal and external problems. At the same time they make every effort to increase the reputation of the Popular Party and its president, A. Mock, who enjoys the full approval of America. It is not a secret that at Washington's recommendation Mock was elected as president of the International Democratic Union (IDU), which aims to become the conservative counterweight of S.I. throughout the world.

It is characteristic that Washington accepted gladly the relative failure of the Socialists in the parliamentary Elections in April, 1983, when they lost the absolute majority and were forced to make a political alliance with the Liberal-National Party of Freedom. Even greater pleasure was expressed by right-wing U.S. politicians when Kreisky vacated the position of Federal Chancellor.

Kreisky's defamation and isolation are continuing to be one of the most important duties of the misinformation services of the CIA. Especially strong is the pressure applied on the leader of Austrian Socialists by the Zionist Lobby of the U.S.A. which exploits in every way the fact that Kreisky, although himself a Jew, refutes zionism and is opposed to the expansion of Israel, while trying at the same time to find a just solution to the Middle East problem which considers the legal interests of the Arab people. A very active role in this, guided by the CIA example, is played by the Israeli Press, which condemns Kreisky as an 'apostate' and 'semi-fascist'. The unworthy intrigues which are used to defame Kreisky are illustrated by the fact that his half-brother Paul, who now lives in Haifa, is being used against him.

The U.S.A. versus Isek of Spain

During the post-Franco (dictatorship) period, the U.S. followed a political line which was intended to support centrists led by Soares, as the only power strong enough to prevent Socialists from pursuing their aim of forming a leftist government led by ISEK. According to the Washington Post (July 30, 1976), American dollars were used to support financially a party connected with reviving the monarchy rather than Franco and the Cival War generation. For this reason the right wing Popular Axis, whose leaders were among the highest in Franco's regime, didn't get the promised financial aid, as their active pre-election campagn could bring about the opposite result and turn the voters towards Socialism.

At the end of the '70's decade when ISEK became an obvious alternative to the Socialdemocrat Party for ruling the country, the USA tried to exert influence on its political line, to give a reforming character to that. The peak of this campaign was reached on the eve of ISEK's extra convention (in September 1979). A CIA agent, Ray Coldwell, an official in the political department of the US Embassy in Madrid, held repeated meetings with the party's instructors, trying to convince them of the expediency of preserving principles which were sympathetic to the strategic interests of Washington.

Trying for a last time to influence Spanish Socialists, the US government didn't give a very warm welcome to ISEK representatives who visited Washington in January 1980, led by A. Guerra (the second most important man in the party). During this visit ISEK representatives had planned to talk with Brzerinski the President's assistant on matters of National Security, to Senator Edward Kennedy and to other government officials. Neither one of these political figures though, had the time to meet with Guerra. As a result of this behaviour ISEK representatives stayed for just a week instead of the planned 20 days, considering their stay to be useless. Washington gave Gonzales to understand that under the existing circumstances his party was not considered worth talking to.

For the last 8 years, the USA has tried to force ISEK to stop criticising American military strategic interests in Spain. According to Kissinger, the basic aim of American diplomacy is 'to avoid any possible neutrality in Spanish foreign policy'.

The main instigator of this trend towards neutrality was ISEK, which in

1976 condemned the plans for further negotiations regarding American military bases. Not accidentally, the most important duty of the CIA team in Madrid, led by R. Ganangen, was 'to prevent neutrality'.

After their victory in the Parliamentary elections in November 1982, according to the Spanish Press, instead of the traditional congratulations the Socialists received from the American government a series of serious warnings against the strict implementation of their pre-election commitment (to get out of NATO and to reconsider their agreement with the U.S.) This last warning was received on the eve of Minister of Exterior Shultz's visit to Spain in December 1982. In Madrid they assume that the USA has strong means of making Gonzales administration amend its policy, such as the support of Morroco's representatives in relation to the cities Seiouta and Melilia, a threat to the re-finacing of the Spanish State's debts, encouragement of Separatists in the Canary Islands and stirring up anti-government feelings amongst the nationalist movements in Catalonia and the Basque land. Recently the U.S. Ambassador, Toadman, has increased his contacts with these movements.

In the U.S. armory these methods of undermining Socialists by applying various pressures has remained unused. Until not it is not clear, where the report which was received by the Socialdemocratic Party's leaders came from. The report alleges that during a visit to Moscow (1977) ISEK signed an 'agreement', which obliged the Socialists to prevent the entrance of Spain into NATO, in exchange for Moscow's support in every other way. It is very possible that this report was made by the CIA.

The USA versus Portugese Socialists

In 1975, during a period of political changes towards democracy in Portugal, in the American Press there suddenly appeared evidence about the financing of Portugese Socialdemocracy by the CIA. This evidence came as a result of a leak of information. At the beginning an announcement was published about the permission that the special services of the U.S. had received in connection with the supply of financial aid to non communist parties in Spain, Portugal and Italy. Right after that the New York Times (May 26, 1975) wrote that American dollars were being given by the CIA to West German Socialdemocrats. This operation was approved by President Ford personally. The announcement was published on the same day by the agency FRANCE PRESS.

This was an attempt to defame not only Soares, but also the whole S.I. presenting the Portuguese leader to the public as an American puppet. It is characteristic that the announcement was not denied by President Ford, although such denials were the usual case in previous similar operations of the CIA. The key to this secret can be found in Senator MacGovern's report on the situation in Portugal: 'Soares denied the rumours that he was taking money from CIA. He understands well the undoubted fact of Portugese policy since 1975: Whoever becomes 'ours' in Lisbon, as a result of CIA's bribery, will be rejected by all the Portugese'. In October 1975, Willy Brandt denied decisively the announcement that he was an agent of the American special services, in an interview which was given to FRANCE PRESS News agency. It is obvious that this enterprise was also aimed at Willy Brandt.

According to Soares, the confirmation of this fact would mean the political assassination of the Socialist Party and its leader.

During the period which came after the so called 'Revolution of carnations' The White House recommended that the CIA arrange in Portugal a series of enterprises intended to create situations which could be used by the Americans to control the political situation in the country through the right wing forces. After the visit of the sub-director of the CIA, General Walters, to Portugal, a new U.S. Ambassador, Karuzzi, arrived in Portugal. He tripled the Embassy's personnel. Two months after Karuzzi's arrival he got involved in the preparation of the unsuccessful coup d'etat of General de Spinola, on March 11, 1975. This was openly stated by one of the leaders of 'Armed forces movement' Ottelo de Carvallio.

'The committee of 40', a State Department team which is employed in especially secret matters, decided on a programme for CIA's active participation which was issued at the beginning of 1975. An important channel used for infiltration by the American special services proved to be through the Church.

It is believed that with the Catholic Church's help the Americans succeeded in making contact with a series of right wing organisations in the northern parts of the country. Between the Portugese Church and the CIA, the American Church and members of the Portugese Community in New England played the role of mediator.

F. Agy, a former CIA official, also said that American intelligence organised a special team of agents, who had previously been active in Latin America (Brazil, Uraguay and Chile) to stir up Catholics in the northern areas of Portugal to make extortionate demands and antigovernment protests. In addition the Americans assisted in the creation of an organisation made up of Portugese Fascist Immigrants with the name 'Portugese Liberal Army'. The duties of the director of this terrorist group were taken by Guerren-Shirac (his real name is Yve Geyou) – a former officer and long time manager of a fake advertising company, AGITER PRESS, in

Portugal, a man connected with the CIA. This company, was used as a cover, both for the coordinating centre of European right wing terrorists and for Hugh Frankli (Sablovsky), an American, who had worked in the worlds hottest spots, immediately before coup d' etats in Chile, Guatemala and Bolivia.

In order to put additional pressure on the new authorities in Lisbon, and also for the protection of American military and strategic interest in the Azores, the U.S. endeavoured to reactivate the local separatist parties, which had actually not been heard of since the end of the last century. An active part in the restoration of relations with these circles was taken by the famous R. Allan, who elaborated the idea of the creation of a Stock exchange centre in the Archipelago in the name of a series of companies. During the revolutionary events in the Azores the media attempted a massive brain wash through both television channels and radio broadcasts of American troops who were stationed in Terseira island and else where.

As a result of this, between the years 1977 and 1978, the 'Front for the liberation of Azores' began open terrorist activities. The escalation of violence in the Archipelago, called by Soares 'a national problem', reduced significantly the ability to manoevre of the Portugese government, especially in negotiations for the future of the American military base in Azores, because the separatists would loudly extol in every way the importance of American aid for the development of the islands, which was given in exchange for their use as a base.

In 1977 Carter's government deliberately didn't supply Mario Soares government with a loan which amounted to 550 million dollars. The DIARO POPULAR newspaper recommended the need to reconsider the social policy of the Portugese authorities, which Socialists usually expected, as much as the need to promote a strictly frugal economy. The newspaper ZORNAL NOVEU, controlled by Portugese business circles assessed this action of the U.S. 'to be a serious warning for the Portugese People and democratic institutions'.

Soares's government found itself in a very difficult situation at the time when it was undertaking serious negotiations to join the EEC. It is obvious that the delay of the promised loan from U.S.A. was politically motivated. Washington tried to force Lisbon to support them even more, in the matter of military cooperation.

Later on, when after a three year period the Socialists regained power in Portugal, they were faced with new and open demands by the U.S. It is clear that the persistent demands of Washington for the concession of continental Portugal's bases to the Pentagon, and the increase in the rights which

American troops have to use Lazice, the military air-force base, are based on the certainty that the Portugese have no alternative to agreement other than bankruptcy. In exchange for the expansion of the American military presence on Portugese territory the U.S.A. were able to promise the provision of aid to Lisbon with grants from the International Monetary Fund, and credits for the amortization of a part of its foreign debts.

Craxi: an appropriate Socialist for Washington

This chapter is based on an article published in the ETHNOS newspaper (August 21, 1983) by the title 'What attracts Craxi in the area'.

To the conservatives who are ruling at the White House, the word Socialist is an insult; but there are some Socialists who are a little bit different to Washington, and one of these rare exceptions is the leader of the Italian Socialists, Bettino Craxi.

Craxi has as his target the pursuit of authority. Christian democrats, who ruled Italy for three decades, lost their influence upon the people. The Communists, who are the second power in the country, do not progress politically.

The Socialist victories in Southern Europe (France, Greece, Spain, Portugal) handed a trump card to Craxi. Craxi called early parliamentary elections in Italy with the hope of gaining benefit from the situation and extracting benefits for his party.

Craxi, though, did everything in such a way that the spectre of Socialist Italy did not scare the Americans. The position of the Italian Socialist Party on more important matters of foreign and internal policy didn't cause Washington any concern.

Even at the beginning the Italian Socialist Party supported Reagan's campaign in relation to 'International Terrorism'. At a time when West Europe, except for the extreme right wing forces, expressed its displeasure and suspicion of the foreign and internal policy of the American government, Italian Socialists supported Reagan completely.

It was obvious that the Italian Socialist's actions and the U.S. government had been coordinated from the very beginning. Claudio Martelli, Craxi's right hand man, was present at the American President's inaugural ceremony and that trip was characterised as 'A journey of hope'.

A french newspaper wrote: 'As a reward for his good services, Craxi hopes to be appointed one day by the White House as President of the Ministerial Council of Italy'. In that Craxi succeeded.

The Italian Socialist Party warmly supported the installation of missiles in Europe and attacked the antiwar movement which grew after the establishment of a military base in Comizo, in Sicily.

Craxi made many efforts to slander the antiwar movement supporters; calling the movement 'fake' and accusing it of anti-americanism. At the same time the Socialists acquired an unexpected ally, the Mafia. The Mafia was not so much pro-American as intent on promoting business. The Comizo bases provided a 'market' for the Mafia. When Americans arrived they liked to have prostitutes and drugs and in that way a black market was established and other profitable business for the Mafia.

The Socialist Party often blindly repeated the Pentagon's and CIA's argument on the matter of the balance of power around the world. There have been published on AVANTI's pages articles on this matter which were first published in the extreme right wing press of the West.

During the last 42nd convention of the Italian Socialist Party, a member of Parliament, Socialist Franco Basanini, said that after a period of time instead of singing the hymn 'International' in the assemblies, Socialists would sing the American Marines Anthem.

However extreme the anticommunism and antisovietism of the American President was, it could be easily imposed on Bettino Craxi. On this question there is not one word or action of the U.S. president which Craxi would not support. Craxi supports all the boycotts, embargos, penalties and restrictions aimed at the U.S.S.R. – for example, the case of the agreement about 'gas-pipes'.

Craxi was not frightened by the inflammatory rhetoric of Ronald Reagan, although a former Socialist president, Perini, had named it 'provocative'.

The Italian Socialist Party's leadership refused to consider the Americans responsible for the bloody incidents in Lebanon and Salvador.

Bettino Craxi was always a loyal ally of Washington on the matter of the participation of Communists in government. According to the New York Times the American Ambassador in Rome, Gartner, considered the widening gap between the Italian Socialist Party and the Italian Communist Party to be one of the greatest successes of his four year service in Italy.

'The relations between Socialists and Communists have never been as bad as today', wrote the American magazine, Foreign Affairs, with admiration. Americans have no reason to be afraid of 'pink' Italian Socialism.

On October 31, 1981 Reuter, the western news agency, wrote that during Craxi's government, Socialists had entirely deserted their Marxist inheritance.

On every matter related to NATO's activity, the USA would find in Europe no more unreserved support for their policy than the support of the Italian Socialist Party's leadership.

The Foreign Affairs magazine wrote that the minister of Defence, Socialist Lelio Latorio, is more faithful to NATO, than any other Christiandemocrat.

The American specialist on Italian affairs, Jojeff La Palobara, said of Craxi's party. 'The position of the Socialist Party on international matters are more coordinated with Reagan's policy than the majority of European left and right wing parties'.

This fact maybe doesn't mean that Americans can now trust Italian Socialists rather than Christian Democrats? De Carolis – *known* Party, understood that the Americans are trying to replace Christian democrats with Socialists in order to ensure a closer cooperation.

Craxi obviously succeeded in his purpose. This representative of left wing forces became a close friend of Washington.

He is the only member of S.I. who gained the confidence of the White House.

How the CIA overthrew the Australian Government

In 1973, in Sydney, the American Commercial Bank, Newgen-Hand, was founded. In 1980 when this bank went bankrupt, it became clear that its personel consisted of former high standing American agents, while amongst its directors were agents of the U.S. intelligence service. In 1981, Robert Inman the former director of the National Security Agency and the deputy director of CIA, declared that any further investigation of this bank would reveal many dirty tricks, a victim of which is Gough Whitlam's government.

In 1972 Gough Whitlam formed a government from the Labour Party. However the first actions of Whitlam, both inside and outside his country, aroused the undisguised displeasure of Nixon's government. Whitlam cancelled Military Service, bringing back all the soldiers from South-East Asia, recognised Cuba, North Korea, the people's Democracy of Germany and eliminated the obstacles to trade with socialist countries. As Henry Olbinsky the recognised American Specialist on Australian – U.S.A. affairs remarked 'even before getting well settled into power, the Australian Labour Party caused serious damage to American-Australian relations'.

The White House's negative attitude towards Whitlam and his government became intolerable when in 1973 the Australian Police revealed some facts about the Australian organisation of Security and Intelligence which were closely connected with the CIA and which were being closely investigated. Following this the names of the CIA agents in Australia were announced in the Australian Parliament.

As was said earlier, Whitlam's actions created a really dangerous situation when it was proved under pressure that not only was top secret information being given by the CIA to Australian Intelligence but their was even further cooperation between the two intelligence services. According to James Engleton the head of the counter-intelligence department of CIA, 'the intelligence of the U.S. couldn't stand aside just in order to avoid a crisis in their relations with Australian Intelligence'.

As proof of the fact that the CIA was not an indifferent observer of the events in Australia, was the ultimatum given by American intelligence to the Australian intelligence. Using an aggressive tone the ultimatum was demanding 'tame Whitlam'.

At the start of 1975, the CIA together with Australian Intelligence formulated a plan which was intended to overthrow Gough Whitlam's government. Mainly they were relying on discrediting his economic policy.

By the order of the CIA, Australian Intelligence, exploiting its connections with the Australian Labour Party, obtained some information regarding Whitlams efforts to obtain a large loan for the Australian Economy which would cover the deficit, which in 1975 was expected to reach the height of 4 billion dollars. Seeking for an appropriate bait, the CIA managed to attract the Australian Labour Party's attention, through the Newgen-Hand bank, to a CIA man named Tirat-Khlemani, a Pakistan banker who lived in Singapore.

Khlemani was ordered to announce the contents of a telex about the progress of economic discussions which were being organised by CIA agent Joseph Flynn, by the order of a former CIA's official, Edwin Wilson. At this point the scandal reached Parliament. During these discussion, violations of a legislative character were made clear. James Kirns, Vice President of the government, and Rex Conner, the Minister of Natural resources who had direct contact with the Pakistani were removed from their positions.

In April 1975 Gough Whitlam stated it was possible that the American-Australian agreement for the U.S. base Pine-Gap on Australian ground would not be renewed. At that time he knew that this American base was in reality a centre of electronic espionage by the CIA and was used as a cover for its agents.

At the end of September 1975, CIA's representatives in the U.S. Embassy in Canberra held repeated meetings with the Governor General, John Kerr – Kerr had maintained close contacts with the CIA from its very start and supported their policies.

Through his contacts with the CI representatives, Kerr was entrusted with the role of 'executioner' of Whitlam in exchange for benefits from the American Government.

On November 10, 1975, one day before the day fixed by Whitlam for talks in Parliament on the subject of CIA's agents, the official position of the CIA was given to the Australian leader. In their ultimatum CIA told him to stop every activity unfavourable to the CIA, otherwise it was threatened that he would face counter-measures.

On November 11, 1975 Kerr, without sending the notice required in these cases to the British Foreign Minister and the Queen, put aside Whitlam and appointed the pro-american leader of the opposition, Malcolm Frazer, as temporary Prime Minister of Australia.

The CIA still works actively against the present government of Australia and its Prime Minister, Labour leader, R. Hawk. At the order of the CIA, the Australian intelligence service gathered adverse information about leading personalitities in the Labour Party. This information is of value to the CIA if ever they wish to repeat the bloodless coup of 1975, in a future emergency,

A short time before the official visit of Robert Hawk, the Australian Prime Minister, to the U.S.A. on June, 1983, Hawk gave a press conference to the American magazine, United States News and War Report, where he made some statements which incurred the displeasure of the U.S. President Ronald Reagan and of Casey, the chief of the CIA. At this conference Hawk said, most specifically, that the committee, organised by himself, would analyse relations between the Australian security and intelligence agency and the CIA. He also expressed the wish that the present day government of the country could be kept closely informed about American espionage centres in Australia.

On June 13 of the same year, during Hawks stay in the USA, the CIA, exploiting its connections with the Washington Post, published an article in which Hawk was characterised as a recent alcoholic, and a man un-disciplined in his personal life. These slanders caused him much damage in the Australian Council of Syndicates, of which Hawk was the president.

Though referred to in this article specific evidence of Hawk's immoral activities never came to light.

Should one consider it coincidental that the slanders against Hawk first came to light at the exact time he was visiting the U.S.A., for the first time, as Australian Prime Minister?

Bearing in mind the fact that the CIA used many ways to combat Socialdemocrats, the Socialist party members of S.I. and the leaders of these parties, we could say with great certainty, if questioned, that this campaign against Hawk was not coincidental but well planned and well prepared.

'A Red Rose for Olaf Palme'

13
CIA's International Campaign of Defamation against Andreas Papandreou, PASOK and Greece

One of the first aims of Imperialism is to fight against 'Socialist International', which pose an obstacle to Imperialism's criminal intentions.

Imperialism however, doesn't just strike at members of S.I., but at all other socialdemocratic and socialist parties which do not belong to S.I. such as the Pan-Helleric Socialist Movement (PASOK) which are considered to be dangerous to the realization of imperialism's dark and secret purposes. Using the usual channels, mainly the CIA, Imperialism penetrates socialist and socialdemocrat parties from all over the world, in order to destroy them, preventing the socialist idea spreading to those it should reach.

It had been proved up to now that imperialist and Zionist agents, mainly from the CIA, work according to long-term programmes which have been elaborated by clever human brains and computers. The methods they use are so devilish that the socialist governments are not able to locate them in time. They also recruit people as agents to further their plans who are so unlikely to be suspected that in many cases they occupy positions such as congressmen, ministers and socialist party executives. The socialist leaders and their associates do not suspect them. Usually they discover them when it is almost too late and put them aside, but by then the damage is done....

PASOK, although as we have said above it is not a member of S.I., is still a target of Imperialism because the socialist transformation, started by Andreas Papandreou and continuing in our country, poses for Imperialists a serious problem. The fact that the Greek Prime Minister achieved for his policy international consideration on many serious and critical matters, such as disarmament, the banning of nuclear weapons, the domination of International peace, the necessity for small countries to be heard in the strident talks between the two Superpowers, the removal of bases and several other points, were enough to make them a target of the imperialists.

If one examines deeply the cancellations, the about turns and the resignations of some PASOK members who served the party as congress men and ministers for a long period of time, and if one researches their background and their hitherto unknown activity in the USA, it can be understood and learnt how Imperialism uses the CIA, how it corrodes the socialist parties and how it corroded, up to a degree, the Greek Socialist party of Andreas Papandreou.

Psychological War

During the last few years the CIA has started a psychological war against the president of PASOK and the Prime Minister of Greece.

This war, as are most enterprises of the CIA, is perfectly planned and organised. It started essentially in 1974 but continued more systematically after 1981.

In order to give the reader a chance to understand the reasons which caused the CIA to organise this war on behalf of the U.S.A., the short historical background given below has to be taken into consideration, always bearing in mind the targets which are: Andreas Papandreou and Papandreou and PASOK.

Andreas Papandreou's party, the Pan Hellenic Socialist Movement (PASOK), was founded in 1974 immediately after the unsuccessful coup d'etat in Cyprus and the fall of the military junta of the Colonels in Greece. The founder of the party, Andreas Papandreou had accused the USA of stirring up the Dictatorship in Greece and the situation in Cyprus, and declared that in the event of his party's victory in the parliamentary elections, he would abolish the USA's bases in Greece and he would lead the country out of NATO.

It is understandable that no other socialist in Europe caused so much concern to the USA as did Papandreou. That is why Washington's reaction to him was proportional.

On the eve of the elections of 1981, which Papandreou won, American press printed many warnings that in the cases of a Socialist victory, private capital investments in Greece would be reduced. Many other problems were predicted for the Greek economy.

On the eve of the Greek elections of 1981 we referred to above, the request of Greek right wing political agents was under examination in the U.S., which was to install American military units in order to 'cool down' the Greek voters. The U.S. Minister of the Armed Forces supported this idea, which however never materialised. Maybe Washington could not bring itself to believe in a Papandreou's victory. Maybe they thought that there were other ways of applying pressure, which could be more effective if PASOK should indeed win the elections. So that's what happened.

The Americans used every means to fight against the Socialist government, threating even a new coup d'etat. The American magazine 'US NEWS and WORLD REPORT' wrote at the beginning of 1983, that in the Greek army, the officers were orientated towards western political systems, so if there was no other way to prevent a further turn by Greece towards the left they could apply something which had been tested previously: The military coup d'etat.

The U.S. intention to recruit the whole opposition against the socialist government was unlimited. 'Secret U.S. intervention causes conflict between Karamanlis and Papandreou'. This was widely announced in May 1983 in the Greek newspaper 'The News'. Let us point out the fact that President of Democracy, K. Karamanlis, was founder and leader of the conservative party, called 'New Democracy', and his main opponent was Andreas Papandreou with PASOK.

Following PASOK's victory and up to that time, Karamanlis and Papandreou had a good relationship and there was no foundation in any of the rumours related to a conflict whch later on occurred. The conflict which was referred to in the newspaper was hatched by the American news agency with which 'The News' at the time had an agreement. The Americans didn't want Karamanlis to use all his power against Papandreou, but they tried to provoke him.

A special opportunity for the USA to use pressure against Papandreou was given during the negotiations between the two countries on the future of American bases in Greece. 'Pressure by any means', 'Suffocative pressure, which takes the form of an ultimatum', 'Extortion', 'Cruel pressure by the USA', these were the headlines in the Greek newspapers (which are close to government), criticising Washington's attempts to impose its terms about the military bases on the Greek people.

For this purpose also, the Turkish factor had been widely exploited. The Americans violated the proportion of provision of military aid towards the two neighbouring countries-allies in NATO. These two 'allies' view each other through gunsights, and under these circumstances Washington preserved the ratio 10:7 (in favour of Turkey) with the purpose of making Papandreou toe the line. Reagan's government changed this proportion even more to the benefit of Evren's junta. However, in April, 1983, obviously fearing the unexpected results of such a policy, Reagan's administration restored the balance to 10:7.

The Turkish factor was used in another way. The Americans showed their support of Evren's Junta in its confrontation with Greece regarding territorial rights in the Aegean Sea. Washington supported Ankaros against Athens, in matters of authority during the NATO military exercises in the Aegean Sea. The U.S.A. were continually violating, together with the Turks, the Greek air space. In March, 1983 the socialist leader of Greece, Andreas

Papandreou, declared, during his visit to Canada, that the U.S. must carry the whole responsibility for the clash between the two countries in the Aegean Sea.

Before the final round of negotiations in January 1983, the statement by the president of the committee which was employed with U.S. foreign affairs Congressman Zablotski, caused a wave of protest in Greece. This audacious American official threatened the Greeks that in the case of the abolition of American military bases on Greek territory the danger from Turkey would be increased. 'The New York Times' wrote in the same spirit: 'If Papandreou persists in this vein it will be beneficial for the other country of the Aegean Sea but not for Greece'.

The U.S.A. also tried to reduce the activity of the Socialist government of Greece internationally. In January 1983 Papandreou told Greek reporters in Paris that President Reagan had asked for the meeting of 7 in Williamsburg to be organised earlier, because Andreas Papandreou could be present as EEC representative in July.

Washington, repeatedly tried to block Papandreou when Greece occupied a special position on a series of foreign policy matters in NATO's forum and elsewhere. One of these matters was, for example, the recent proposition of Athens regarding the postponement of the installation of American Euro-missiles.

If we now add to these few things, the known initiatives of Papandreous for a missile-free Balkans, even without the participation of Turkey, and also his position as a member of the team of 'Six' against nuclear armament, everybody can easily understand the reasons for this psychological war waged by the U.S., through the CIA, against Papandreou and PASOK.

By Many Means

This war uses many different means in our own land, as well as abroad, by people or groups of people with or without a political background who consciously or unconsciously are 'recruited for this war operation'.

The 'methods of war' usually employed by the mercenaries of the CIA (both by the paid associates or those people unconsciously involved in CIA's war) are the media, news agencies, radio and T.V. stations, video-tapes, magazines, newspapers and books.

In Greece, there are books attacking PASOK and Papandreou written by the following authors: Botsaris, Mylonas and Hondrokoukis. Video tapes have been made by Karatzaferis, and the 'Free Press' newspaper, through its editor, Voudouris who has a leading role in the war against the Greek Prime Minister and his party.

A Disgraceful Book

For the time being though we will not discuss the people referred to previously. We should rather discuss a foreign book with an extremely defamatory content against Papandreou, called 'Euroterrorism' and sub-titled 'The smothered Belgium', authors of which are Jac Offergeld, a Jew and Souris, a Greek Christian, both of whom now have Belgium Citizenship.

This book was printed in Belgium in the French language in December 1985 and it started to circulate in the beginning of 1986 through the publishing company 'SCAILLET'. Its prologue is written by Pier Grozen, Honourary Professor of Mons University and has the indicative title: 'Carl Marx and Allah had the same target: Death to the West'.

This professor in his ten page prologue develops the theory of the U.S. foreign ministry (State Department) and of the CIA, describing the 'ten war fronts' of East against West through International Organisations: the International Students Union, the International Federation of Democratic Youth, the Universal Federation of Scientists, the Democratic Lawyers, the Democratic Reporters etc.

'It is known world wide – (Grozen says) – that the USSR has penetrated Socialist International, The Peace Council, the Universal Council of Churches, the United Nations, and its branches, such as UNESCO...'

Referring to 'exports' like Clair Sterling, a known associate of the CIA, and Zan Francois Revel, a Jewish Zionist, the Professor alleges that behind all these people is Moscow and its satellites. First comes Bulgaria, (the case of the umbrella and the assassination attempt against the Pope), and right after comes Greece, which is, according to the book 'the most obviously active ally of the USSR with Socialist Papandreou's blessings'. In this book the professor refers to East Germany as a third satellite.

He (Professor Grozan) writes specifically in pages 9 and 10: '...of course Greece is not a satellite like Bulgaria or Cuba. But if we consider its anti-american feelings and its inbred hatred of Turkey which is a privileged member of EEC, so Greece is the most obvious country to be expected to be an ally of the USSR. We must remember the fact that when the Belgium Minister of the Exterior Leo Tintemans, negotiatcd with NATO's allies the plan for a fast development of European missiles, there was only one dissenting vote: the vote of Greece... Besides Greece maintains an open friendship with the Arabs. We are not surprised by the fact that Athens took precedence of Beirut as head quarters of the terrorists, who are already gathered in ten well known organisations.

We name these without any special order as: Islamic Group of Action,

Black September, Black June, Arabic Action against Americans, Iraq mission against Iran, Homeinis Victims, Muslim fighters against Allah's enemies, and also three other organisations which belong to the PLO. We must not forget these organisations, the existence of which the police suspect but are almost unable to take measures against... When the Seights diverted the TWA aeroplane at the end of June, 1985, the weakness of the Greek police was proved completely: The terrorists took off from Athens without any difficulty, together with their guns and luggage. The foothills of Acropole are a true terrorist paradise, with the blessings of the socialist, Papandreou. That's why the CIA was forced to impose order with the usual way: it organised attacks against some shelters of the terrorists in the city of Athens with shots and victims (a Syrian and a Moroccan), the arresting of a Palestinian and his British girlfriend, as well as some Arabs of different origin, cleaning up their arsenal and seizing 350 kilos of explosives. And it is useless to say that 'the terrible Americans' were punished rightly by the good Papandreou. And at the end he apologised to his Arab friends...'

In the ninth chapter of that book the 'reticent allies' of terrorism are numbered. According to the author among Castro, Kadhaffi and Assad are included people like Papandreou and Dom Mindoff. Specially tough are the attacks against Papandreou, whom, the authors allege, fully supports the foreign policy of the Soviet Union, and under who's leadership Greece had been converted into a den of terrorists, including the members of the secret organisation of the Armenians 'Assala'.

Specifically in pages 120-123 he writes: '... If Kadhaffi, Castro, Assad and some others are known as supporters of international terrorists, there are other states or government officials, who though more restrained never the less manage to be allies of the terrorists, and we must not ignore them. It is specially important to keep our attention on these two: the Greek, Andreas Papandreou, and the Maltese, Dom Mintoff.

Officially Papandreou is president of PASOK, the Panhellenic Socialist movement. This organisation is not a member of Socialist International and it is reasonable to expect them not to associate with terrorist circles. In spite of all this, after he fled from Beirut, Yassar Arafat landed at Athens.

There he was welcomed with the honour which is reserved only for a State official. The Greek Prime Minister Andreas Papandreou, accepted him and kissed him in public, treating him as a very close friend.

In the old days, before Socialists came to power, Athens was even then 'the gate' of Europe, and one of the most notorious centres of international terrorism. When Papandreou took over, the situation became worse. Thus the PLO has an official diplomatic representation, which, it would seem,

122

undertakes activities which have nothing in common with the provision of the Vienna convention.

Sometimes, as has been known, terrorists are boarding aeroplanes which are in transit through the Greek capital. Any action which follows make the police appear as blind, deaf and dumb cripples.

In reality though, there is no doubt that terrorists have significant support in Greece. In 1983 a Greek told us the following in confidence: 'It is true that some of the younger members of PASOK in my country sympathise with the Palestinian struggle and have tried to help the International terrorists who found asylum in Greece.

In the framework though, of International agreement with which we should comply, we tried to locate these undesirable terrorists and to throw them out of our country. We made many arrests, many other persons were being watched and we opened many files. With Papandreou now in government things have changed rapidly. First of all, the outstanding Police officers, especially those who were known for their effective actions against terrorism, either became retired prematurely or have been transferred to insignificant duties in the countryside. Their positions were taken by incompetent people who were, however friendly towards the government. Their role was not to chase terrorists but to offer them their aid. Thus I can say that sometimes Cyprian passports were brought from Cyprus which had all the necessary seals of approval, and they were given to Palestinians.

I am not interested in politics and I was not concerned about the change of government, just continued with my work. One day though an associate came to my office and said to me: 'You don't understand what's happening. We cannot cause any trouble for the Palestinians or the members of the Red Brigade. If you have any sense you will not keep watching those people while at the same time our congressmen and members of PASOK are welcoming them'.

The sycophants of Papandreou and PASOK then continued with the following words which I choose selectively because I cannot, of course, copy the whole book:

'Thus, it becomes obvious that in this situation Greece has been changed from a barrier to the terrorist, to a summer resort which allows them to enjoy the sun while they work.

And it is also true that all this will not sound strange to your ears, if you bear in mind Papandreou's foreign policy, which is completely parallel with Moscow's. That's why Greece was the only country-member of EEC which did not condemn, indeed actively approved, the invasion of the Red Army in

Afghanistan, and was the only country which made a plan of unilateral disarmament in the Balkans. Also Greece was reluctant to criticise the assassination of the Korean Boeing 747 passengers by the Soviet air force in September 1983.

The Greek Prime Minister is not satisfied by the fact that he provides significant help to the Palestinian terrorists, but is also supporting the Armenians. That's why his foreign ministers issued a circular letter, which ordered the immediate supply of residence permits to every Palestinian citizen of Armenian origin. It is obvious that such a measure was a blessing to the people of 'ASSALA', and they used this hospitality to establish strategic bases in Athens to such a degree that today there exists in the city about twenty centres 'welcoming the incoming Armenians'. Our police official contact points out that it is prohibited to search these centres or to watch any people entering or leaving them.

Our colleague, Rolan Zakar, also alleges that there is a laboratory which makes forged identification cards and passports in the suburbs of Athens. Thus a man known as **Monde Mikonian,** who was arrested on November 11, 1981, had a forged passport in the name of George Dimitriou which was supplied by this laboratory.

The relations between Athens and Tripoli are getting closer every day. On this matter the weekly newspaper, 'Le Poin' on August 18, 1985 reveals in a column marked 'confidential': 'The government of West Germany found itself in a very difficult situation when Libya bought from Greece, the super-modern aerial technology, called 'Artemis'. This is a system of location made by the 'Siemens' company, which was given to Greece. Without informing anybody and without observing the elementary rules banning the re-exportation of super-sensitive technology, they resold it to Kadaffi. 'Artemis' is the name of one of the most modern counter-missile systems in NATO defence. The experts were enraged at the mere thought that 'KGB' specialists could examine and study this system in Tripoli at their leisure'.

These and many more are the slanders which are written by the authors referred to above in 'Euro-terrorism', which because of its titles, subject and language, has a circulation of many thousands of copies.

The foreign reader of course, ignoring the motivation and the purpose of the authors of these books, who carry the pompous titles of University Professors, can easily form the wrong idea and the political image of Andreas Papandreou or PASOK, which is at present the ruling party of Greece, is destroyed and our country defamed. All this comes about just because they want us to be another Banana Republic, slaves of American

Imperialists and Zionists, and they wish us to sign an agreement which will allow the military bases to stay in our country for another century.

Papandreou, the 'Naughty Boy' of Nato, whose initiatives they find so disturbing

In 'Avriani' newspaper on October 5, 1986, the following article (which now makes a chapter of my book) was published on the eve of the municipal elections, with the known (not so pleasant) result, which unfortunately emphasises my point regarding the 'direct action' against Andreas Papandeou and PASOK, taken according to the CIA's plans.

The reader should pay special attention to this chapter, because it is based on a CIA report concerning PASOK and the recent municipal elections in Greece, in which the American secret service was proved to be very active.

Its subtitle in 'Avriani' (under the above title of the same chapter), was: 'The reason why the Americans are trying to reduce Papandreou's election potential – They react against his idea of declaring the Balkans to be a nuclear-free zone, and to his plan to reduce the American military presence in Greece'.

The Recent Municipal Elections in Greece

The Greek municipal elections on October 12, 1986, even though they were of domestic concern with no immediate political importance, occupied for a long time our 'allies' of NATO, especially the USA, which employed for this purpose CIA's supporters in Athens.

The target of the Special plan, which had been formulated by the heads of the American secret service and part of a wider plan was the socialist government of PASOK and, personally, the Greek leader Andreas Papandreou.

Papandreou, who has been characterised as the 'naughty boy' of NATO, causes much concern to our 'allies' with his initiatives which are known to have effect beyond the Greek borders.

They react, specifically, not only to Papandreou's idea of a nuclear-free Balkans but also to his plan for the reduction of the American military presence in Greece, also they react against his general initiatives for peace and disarmament which are discussed with the 'Six'.

That is why the Americans are trying to reduce PASOK's strength in the municipal elections of October 12, 1986, believing that in this way they will stop the, to them, unfavourable course of the Greek leader. They hope that an increase in power of the right-wing parties will force him to compromise and 'raise a mortgage' for the forth coming Greek municipal elections.

A serious agreement between the USA and the Soviet Union on disarmament matters, would enable Greece, which is in a strategic position on the borders of the two Coalitions, to trust its security to the Americans and to reduce its efforts to secure freedom from the hazzard of war in the world, and especially in this area.

Even though something like this would be difficult to achieve nowadays, Andreas Papandreou correctly intended to continue his initiatives for peace and disarmament, initiatives which reach beyond the Greek borders and appeal to International Common Sense.

Expressing the restlessness of the Greek people and their ruffled feelings about the USA's attitude towards national interests, particularly in relation to Turkey, Andreas Papandreou became active in foreign policy.

His successful international stand, together with the 'Six', for the reduction of nuclear weapons, his later actions following the U.S. attack on Libya, during which American bases in Europe were used, together with his friendly negotiation with the east, particularly the recent ones with Bulgaria, has greatly disturbed our 'allies' in NATO, most especially the Americans.

Nuclear-Free Balkans

The Americans are greatly concerned about the idea of the Greek leader to declare the Balkans a nuclear-free zone. Every postponement of this happening serves the interests of the enemies of our country, especially Turkey, which motivated by other factors, is ready to do everything possible to prevent the realisation of this idea just because the idea originates from Greece.

Turkey's argument, that the nuclear-free zone can be created within the framework of a general agreement between East and West is obviously intended to frustrate the realisation of the idea, because under today's conditions such an agreement seems impossible.

The success of the creation of a nuclear-free zone in the Balkans, would, without any doubt, help the progress of this matter in Northern Europe and will inspire his followers with new hope of a nuclear-free zone and will eventually provide new motivation for further efforts in this direction. The outcome for our country would be to greatly enhance its reputation at an international level.

That's why this effort should start to get under way immediately, without involving Turkey or anyone else who thinks that he is not yet ready.

The Americans know well the intentions of Papandreou with regard to this serious matter and the CIA in a report from Athens to its headquarters points out: '... In the files of Greece's foreign policy there are two plans which are directed towards a total release of the country from its participation in dangerous war preparations. The first plan requires the creation of a nuclear-free zone in the Balkans (and obviously in the future this zone will also exclude chemical weapons and weapons of bacteriological war), and the second plan requires the reduction of the American military presence on Greek soil.

PASOK officials infer that it would be good if, in the future, the files could include one more plan, which would reduce the level of Greek participation in the nuclear programmes of the West, and which would involve the idea of the creation of a missile-free constitution in the country. For this purpose it could be suggested that, at the appropriate moment, a decision of non-participation in the works of the nuclear planning team of NATO, could be taken, or as a first step, non-participation in the next meeting of the team. We would say that this action is compatible with the principles of Greek foreign policy and from Greece's point of view would further the case for a reduction of the nuclear hazzard in Europe and the whole world, and that such a policy would be supported by Greek people'.

The Success of the Group of 'Six' and the 'Small Europe'

The success of the moves of the 'Six' and the creation of a 'Small Europe', has also exercised and annoyed our overseas 'allies'.

That's what the CIA's report also observes, saying '... The success of the activity of the group of 'Six' raises the thought of the usefulness of such activity in the framework of the western alliance.

The strategic targets would follow the same course which follows the initiative of the small countries of Europe, an initiative which turns towards the reduction of danger of war both in Europe and the rest of the world.

This is clearly not obligatory within NATO's framework. Towards this idea could be attracted some neutral countries, which would prevent the accusations of 'undermining the unity' of NATO etc. These initiatives could be taken in two ways – as a multi-faceted character to be used as a governmental political party lever or as a lever of Social agents. A social convention could be organised, for example, which would have as its theme the role of small countries in the political processes of Europe.

It is apparent that Greeks could find followers of the reactivation of 'A Small Europe', not only in the small countries. As a result of similar work, the idea would be supported by valid parties in larger countries e.g. the German Socialdemocrats and the British Labour Party.

We should not exclude the communist parties of Eastern Europe from such participation'.

The Evolution of Pasok and the Conflict between Greece and Turkey

The CIA, which apparently closely monitors PASOK's circles, the Greek government and Papandreou himself, finishes its report which had been made prior to the municipal elections on October 12, 1986 with the following observations: '...From the point of view of internal policy the materialisation of the proposals of the progressive left wing group inside PASOK, will contribute to the union of the party and of its voters and the loss of members and followers will be stopped.

We talk about the difficulties which PASOK faces during the implementation of its wonderful visions. This argument cannot deter the party for a long time, which emerges as a strong, long-term power and not as a transient party, like many others which were around in the country, because, even while moving towards power, PASOK didn't count on the support of any exterior forces, for its was sure that these forces would react against the aims of the movement instead, exerting all possible pressure. That's why in the long-term interests of PASOK, obviously the conseqences of its proposed policy has to be declared and also a resoluteness has to be shown during its execution, without creating the illusion to the opponents that they would be able to prevent the movement completing its programme.

The conflict between Turkey and Greece was used to apply pressure on the members of the alliance. The idea of inviting troops or U.N. observers to some areas of the Greek-Turkish borders (to separate islands or to the most sensitive points of the land borders in Thrace), has to be examined.

Evidence is given that Turkey recently made a series of provocative actions against Greece and threatened its national interests, that it continues, systematically to violate Greek air space and that these actions are not condemned by the allies, although Greece is also a member and the allies are obliged on a collective base to guarantee the security of Greece. In addition, violation of Greek Air Space was committed by another member of NATO – the United States of America.

This idea – according the specific PASOK's group always – could be used in different ways:

– From social point of view, as a social initiative.

– In parliamentary talks or in the Prime Minister's speech.

– Officially in the Security Council of the U.N. observers, which possibly will be rejected by the alliance's side.

It is also sure that this proposal will not be approved by the Security council, because of the U.S. veto (also Great Britain's), but the seriousness of their intentions and the reservedness of the Greek government would be understood by the allies.

These actions will remove the Aegean problem from within the framework of the internal problems of NATO, as it will be considered of world interest and they will elevate it to an international problem. Besides, they will strengthen a Common Sense approach to the demands of Turkey, demands which are contrary to the provisions of International Law'.

A Small Conclusion of Great Importance

A small conclusion, though one of great importance, which I believe that the reader will easily reach is that:

Papandreou really anoys our allies in NATO especially the Americans, which is why they lose no chance that they may have to strike him from behind. Even if they refer to him as a 'friend' they don't trust him absolutely in the critical problems with which they are employed because his intiatives for peace and the abolition of nuclear weapons have started to cause big 'headaches' not only inside NATO, but also inside the United States.

A photograph from the advertising material of the movie 'Delta Force' with evidence which proved the Jewish-American origin. This movie, which was released recently in the cinemas of Athens, was aimed against Greece and Andreas Papandreou while purporting to be a film about a terrorist action.

Jewish-American Production which is Antagonistic to Greece is released in the Movie-Theatres of Athens

Amongst the means which are used by American secret services in order to achieve their ultimate aims, is included the cinema.

Through this massive media the CIA strengthen its 'special campaigns' in matters of general interest and strikes the 'enemy' intermediately, but effectively, at the given moment.

Using the cinema as a weapon of psychological war, CIA spreads the messages which it desires to be known outside of its own American area (also, inside America of course), in such a way that these apparently 'innocent' attacks against their chosen target produce terrific results. That acquires terrible significance if we accept the theory supported by special scientists and psychologists that a man who watches a movie in darkness, has the message of the movie firmly impressed in his mind and soul.

Because I refered above to the term 'Special scientists', I want to remind you that the CIA uses many of those, as many as the other secret services, mainly of the bigger countries. CIA, though, as the major secret service around the world, numbers amongst its numerous personnel a big and various number of Special Scientists, in every field and speciality, who are used to supply their brilliant ideas and their knowledge to further the plans and programs which are elaborated and applied. I had the opportunity to meet a man who was working for the CIA as a scientist. His field was naval architecture. He explained to me why and how the CIA needs the special scientists, who, of course, are very well paid.

'Here in Greece (he said) as well as in other countries, the meaning of the term, CIA's associate, has been misunderstood. When someone hears about CIA's agents he thinks of them as if they were stool-pigeons or informers. Of course CIA have people of this kind, but these are of the lowest rank. In the highest level there are people with brains and knowledge. In order to become a CIA agent you have to be a person with many qualification or talents.

This man was a close associate of Oppenheimer, and they built together the first American nuclear submarine and, of course, the CIA paid them well when they succeeded in putting the big and awkward nuclear reactors into the limited space of an underwater vessel. He was the same man who was placed in the Shipyards of Syros in order to observe the soviet ships which were under repair, but later on he left rather than accept the order of the, then, chief of DIA in Athens, the now departed Chantes (who was murdered in Kifisias Avenue), to take photos of those ships for him, something which seemed to him to be humiliating.

The Movie and its Message

The Movie, which was released in the leading cinema's of Athens during the recent municipal elections, was called 'Delta Force' and had as its subject the known hijack of the American TWA airoplane in Ellinikon airport by an Arab terrorist group. This was the event that triggered the hostile attitude of President Reagan against Greece, with his notorious decision to 'advise' American tourists to avoid Greece.

How much this 'advice' cost Greek tourism and our economy is widely known. However, apart from the economic matter, it caused an equally significant political damage to Papandreou's government and the moral humiliation of Greece internationally.

Of course this 'advice' was revoked later on, but the enormous damage to Greece was already done.

Right after the hijack referred to above, CIA's leaders enlisted the specialists who were available in the field of cinema, Jewish in most part, and started to elaborate the plan for the creation and production of the movie. A movie, the subject of which is political rather than just entertaining, like the famous 'Rambo', which is extremely defamatory towards Greece, because the scenario presents both the Greeks and Arabs as cowards, evil and

130

dangerous, and depicts the representatives of the Greek authorities as incapable and indifferent towards terrorism.

The short 'synopsis' which was distributed by the import company called 'Prospective', (Koletti str. 40–42 3d floor tel. 3644541) tells the following:

'When the American government meets problems with terrorist groups which it is impossible to overcome by negotiations they ask for help from Delta Force. This is a special department of commandos which is used only when the ordinary army cannot get involved. So, when a Boeing 707 gets captured with hundreds of hostages, Major Scott McCoy (Chuck Norris) and Lieutenant Nick Alexander, (Lee Marvin) and their men set out on a mission which seems impossible...

FILM: Coloured.

PRODUCTION: American.

PRODUCING COMPANY: CANNON GROUP 1986.

DIRECTORS: Menahem Golan-James Brunner.

DIRECTOR OF PHOTOGRAPHY: David Gurfinkel.

MUSIC: ALAN SILVESTRI.

STARRING: Chuck Norris, Hanna Sigula, George Kennedy.

As the reader finds out, the 'synopsis' doesn't tell us, for obvious reasons, the specific case of hijack and especially where it took place, which of course is Athens airport.

So the 'competent' Greek authorities didn't notice what the movie was about and gave permission to import it and show it in the following cinemas in Athens: 'Achilleus', 'Astron', 'Titania', 'Lito', 'Tropical', 'Dalia', 'Foebus', and also 'Kapitol' and 'Alfa', of Piraeus from the middle of October, 1986.

This movie presents the Arabs as cruel assassins, while Jews are the eternal victims. Some references were made to their extermination in Hitler's concentration camps. It was filmed in Israel where the Greek airport was reconstructed as a filmset.

It is unnecessary to point out that the creators and producers of this film are American Jews, who, as it is known, control all the media channels (Radio, T.V., etc) as well as companies which produce and distribute films. Producers, scenario writers, directors and other agents are all mainly Jewish.

However, because I don't just want to give my opinion which would be a one-sided criticism of the film, I reproduce here the relevant critique of the well known cinema critic, Mr. N. Fenel-Michelidis:

'Regarding this particular movie we would not be bothered to write about it if there had not been 'Rambo' last year with its political rather than entertaining story which brought this to mind. The story of the new movie is based on the known hijack of the American aeroplane which took place at Hellinikon airport instigated by a group of Arab terrorists, which resulted in turning President Reagan against our country and his advice to American tourists to avoid our country...

The 'Cannon' company, headed by Menehem Golan, one of its founders, who directed this movie, presents us with a scenario politically reactive from every point of view, where everybody except Americans and Israelis are presented as bad, cowardly and irrelevant. Their purpose is to present an adventure where the bravery of the Americans (from 'Delta Force') who undertake the operation of releasing the hostages (the whole movie was filmed in Israel...) is praised, where the Arab terrorists are presented as cruel assassins and the Jews are always victims (with some reference to Hitler's concentration camps...). On the other hand, there are no serious efforts by these makers to analyze deeply the terrorist phenomenon and eventually the only thing that this movie does is to insult the public intelligence'.

It is not necessary to stress the amount of damage which has been done to our country by this movie, which even if (as the critic says) it insults public intelligence, still succeeds in spreading its message, which is the defamation of Greece, and in this way serves excellently the purpose of the CIA.

Also, when we think of how many millions of people will see this movie around the world, for it will continue to be shown for a long period of time, then we can understand the size of the damage and defamation of Greece, even if only fifty percent of the audience understand the message which is turned against Greece, its government, the authorities and all Greeks in general.

The movie 'Delta Force', disregarding its non existant artistic value as a film, belongs in the category of commercial propaganda films which are specially designed to be watched by a large number of people, who, unsuspecting, receive the message which the film cleverly contains.

The only message in this case is one of slander against Greece internationally, striking from many sides.

The 'advice' of the American President Reagan against Greece has of course been revoked, but through this film its spirit continues and the continuing purpose of the CIA is being accomplished, which is why this movie was made in the beginning.

14
Pasok and Papandreou are under attack, by their former Party's Officials

In 1972 for almost one and a half years I had the fortune, (or the misfortune) to work with a group of Greek-Americans, who formed an enterprising partnership working with different projects in Television, co-operating in the beginning with Nikos Mastorakis but later on, following economic and other kinds of disagreements with him, this partnership ceased.

This group, with the dentist Ernest Panos at its head, was then making for the T.V. channel of the Armed Forces, the childrens programme 'BOZO' and at the same time the programme 'Invitation to dinner' for ERT T.V. with Spyros Spridis, later on General Director of ERT 1 as producer and chief editor. Dimitris Katsimis and many reporters, amongst them Spyros Karatzaferis, Costas Tsaruhas and several other working for newspapers and magazines.

I could not work as a reporter because 'Ikones' and Mesimbrini', both published by Vlahou had been closed down, and I was working on the public relations side of these T.V. productions. I was however kicked out because I refused to allow the external broadcasting unit of the company to film a programme on the 'National Government' and because the military personnel officials of YENED, Jaydas and Kitsinelis, together with the 'Minister of Defence' at the time Latsoudis, (an uncle of the company's lawyer, Papandimitriou,) had discovered that I had a record as a communist in the Police Department of Heraklion of Crete. I passed through a series of misadventures, with serious personal effects as Spyros Spyridis and Alkis Steas, who were working together with the Greek-Americans, would not help me, but the 'ΜΕΤΑ-ΝΟΛΙΤΕΥΣΗ' which occured in between put an end to my adventures.

I learned a lot and I met many people and I understood their role during that era of dictatorship, and gained enough material for another book.

At that time the head of the team at the company's offices which were located behind the 'Hilton', introduced me to a newly arrived friend of his from Chicago, with whom to make a new T.V. programme, as a fellow country man of the General Director of ERT (a Junta's officer). If I remember correctly, this cooperation would be a production about atheltics. Dionos Ventikos with whom they had business lunches twice, once in 'John's Inn' in Kypseli and a tavern after Stavros of Agias Paraskevis, would cover it as a reporter.

The man who came from the U.S. 'with special knowledge and high connections' as he was introduced to me by the Greek-American, became, later Andreas Papandreou's favourite friend, Mayor of Spata and a PASOK congressman. He was Dimos Botsaris, but I didn't judge him to be a good person, because one day he came into the company's offices and told me, smiling in a cruel way, about the political prisoner in ESA, who was according to Botsaris arrested as 'An Enemy of the establishment'. Botsaris told me all this information came form the office of his friend Goris'.

Around 1976, if I remember correctly, one afternoon in the hallway of Parliament House, I was talking with our fellow-country men and PASOK congressmen Thanasis Scoulas and Manolis Hatzinakis, and also with their associate Stefanos Joumakas, to whom they introduced me at the time. In a little while Dimos Botsaris, also at that time a congressman of PASOK came, and, as soon as I saw him, I said loudly, in order that he should hear me:

'How is it possible for this man to be a PASOK congressman – that means a socialist?'

Botsaris didn't react and left. Joumakas however reacted for him, telling me that I didn't have the right to talk like that, inside Parliament House, about a trustworthy congressman of the PASOK movment'.

Of course after the events which followed, Jumakas was to change his mind about Botsaris and he would regret that comment as would other members of PASOK, primarily Andreas Papandreou, whose previous friend, confidant and fellow party official has for a long time since changed into an enemy and slanderer of Papandreou and his party.

Dimos Botsaris after his expulsion from PASOK, founded the publishing house 'Isokratis'. Its address is Valaoritou 9, Athens 10671, ph. 3601734, through which he publishes and circulates both his own books and those of people who have a common target: Papandreou and PASOK.

The books which have been published by 'ISOKRATIS' and were written by Botsaris are:

'I reveal the heads of PASOK', 'Papandreou's dynasty', PASOK-SECRET FILE No 1', 'A whisky for Mr President', 'Sartzetaki's case' and 'The big fraud' (Vol. 1).

Books written by others but published through 'ISOKRATIS' are: 'The invisible side of PASOK' by Dim. Hondrokoukis, 'Sink ... the country' by the same author, 'I denounce Andreas Papandreou' by Thalis Mylonas, 'Andreas and we – Documents which whip', by Andreas Kokevis, 'The political heritage of Georgiou Papandreou and Andreas' resistance' by John Voultepsis.

They also have published politically reactive books which are not aimed directly against Papandreou and PASOK but indirectly strike their progressive ideas and movements: I turned down 'The thrill of Aris Velouhiotis' by Dim. Hondrokoukis also by the same author. 'The true Markos Vafiadis' and 'Zahariadis: His bloody journey to Greece'. In addition there is 'The unknown tragedy of Alekos Panagoulis' by John Voultepsis and 'The revelation of Fascism' by the same author.

It has to be pointed out that all the above authors began their political career from the Center and advanced their political career from the centre using its progressive political space, and that all of them, except Voultepsis, were Papandreou's associates.

Voultepsis was never a politically responsible person. He began on the left but finally ended up on the right as a reporter who was sticking with politicians. Now he works in Mitsotakis office for the Press.

Kokevis is on old official of the Center who was once a minister, but during that time he changed from a trustworthy democrat to a server of reactionary right wing interests.

Hondrokoukis and Mylonas were, the first a PASOK official the second almost a congressman, who were seduced by their associates and the publisher Botsaris in order to strike Papandreou and his Socialist Party.

The striking points about this story is that Hondrokoukis was drawn from the extreme right wing and a supporter of the fallen King, while Mylonas later developed relations with American Senators who, before his departure from PASOK, refused to recognise him.

Through these books Dimos Botsaris and the people who follow his ideas have organised a campaign against the people who are in power now in Greece.

Botsaris had pursued this slanderous campaign against PASOK and Papandreou through a series of systematic articles in right wing newspapers, such as 'Akropolis', but mainly in 'Eleftheros Typos', which have been distributed widely to the Greek public.

Apart from this, whether it is true or not what, from time to time, Botsaris and his associates have published about Andreas Papandreou, his family close associates and PASOK, the damage has been done up to a point,

135

because we have to admit that the campaign has been organised according to American standards and it is following its planned path.

Botsaris, who had lived for many years in Chicago, U.S.A. shows in this way that his activity was not reduced only to selling 'hot-dogs' and to being entertained by both sides, (as the gossip says), but he also learned a lot of things in the field of information and misinformation, as well as many secrets about cold war tactics.

But let us not charge only Botsaris or any 'Botsaris' with the whole responsibility (according to my poor judgement) but also Papandreou himself and the top officials of PASOK, who by trusting him, put him in positions and offices from which he could fight them.

Those referred to above are not the only ones. There is also the case of Gerasimos Arsenis, who after four years in sensitive and responsible positions which had been provided for him by the Prime Minister, proved to be a 'wrong choice', showing that in the case of one more 'American-educated' person, Papandreou had made a mistake.

Another is the Alexakis case. He, who was once the highly 'trusted' official of the Central Information Service (KYP), was even more characteristic because by the 'Krystallis' case it was proved that even with PASOK in power the Greek Information Service was cooperating with the CIA.

Such 'wrong moves' on the political chessboard later on unfortunately prove dangerous or fatal, because they give an opportunity to the opponent to eventually win the game.

These misjudgements of people which have been refered to above, and for many others, the sad results of which have not yet surfaced, are the only things for which Papandreou may some day have to find an excuse.

Epilogue

About the time this book was printed for the first time in Greek at the beginning of November 1986, two significant events obscured the political heavens of Greece like two gray clouds.

The first was the turmoil which was caused by the unsuccessful 'new' reformation of Andreas Papandreou's government which was done as a counter-weight to the failure of PASOK in the municipal elections of the previous month. The second was the major scandal which broke, just twenty-four hours later, caused by the transfer of a bank to the Greek-American G. Koskotas.

No one could ever find out how a simple employee of the Bank of Crete bought the bank, or how he found the huge amount of money needed, arriving suddenly on the Greek economic scene buying banks and publishing magazines, and, as Koskotas himself declares, planning to circulate besides his four publications, a hundred-page newspaper and to establish his own private T.V. station.

Behind these two incidents, there is a Zionist-American 'invisible' hand and here is why:

The brains of Zionist-American imperialism, which was such a great help in the accession of the right wing party in the recent Greek municipal elections, (which was not so difficult after government mistakes), applied some pressure on people who have control in the closed circle of the Greek Prime Minister, with dexterity and forcefullness, so Andreas Papandreou, in that difficult time when he was making his decisions for the reformation of the government, got a 'short circuit' and he didn't exploit correctly the message he got from the result of the elections.

Andreas Papandreou, knowing for himself fact and situations from his twenty year stay in the U.S.A. and having also had bad past experiences from his father, George Papandreou's day, preferred to bow to the pressure of Jewish-Americans who used this critical time to issue him, politely with their orders and threats. He knows very well how easy it is going to be for them to realise those threats as they can afford almost everything, at any cost, and they manipulate Turkey's decisions on the Cyprus and Aegean Sea. Also because they pull the strings of the puppet known as Evren's junta.

Andreas, more then anybody else in Greece, knows that because of the matter of his proposed removal of American military bases the Americans would do anything in order to get him to change this decision, thus allowing them to stay in Greece, and especially in Crete. So, by considering the

137

unfavourable climate which was created as a result of the elections and the psychological defeatism of the democrats, by counting the mistakes of his associates, and by thinking about the consequences of a radical reformation which the people demanded and of which he himself, approved, he didn't dare to do it. Neither did he do what the people wanted and for which he had raised lots of hopes, because he was afraid of a possible breaking up of the party, which was almost certain to happen in PASOK when the reformation swept some people away, something which would make even more PASOK members unhappy than the number of people who had already been disappointed. If, after the sweeping away, even one disappointed group left PASOK, then everything would dissolve in the government's galaxy. It would not be necessary for there to be many of these people because, as is known, the government majority inside Parliament is based on a one-digit number. Also the members who would leave couldn't be represented to the people as 'traitors' because of the known general political situation and also because of the personal responsibilities of some former PASOK officials, like Arsenis, who were given so much authority in the past, for a long period of time.

If such a decision were made, it was mathematically certain that with the Analogic electoral system missing, the right wing party would win the elections and the way for the American bases would be clear and covered with flowers.

The second sad incident, the scandal which coincided with the reformation, was about the buying out of the Bank of Central Greece with American dollars, which the newspaper 'Ethnos' dared to report as being supplied by the Mafia. This scandal showed that inside PASOK there are some party officials who are attracted to dollars regardless of the source. Andreas Papandreou himself, who ended this terrible scandal personally, talked about 'fraud' and looked around to find who among his associates had been bribed and who took the 'commission' of 500 million (maybe more) in a similar case of D.E.I. (Nationalisation of Electrical Power).

This fact shows more clearly that, even now, fortunately for the Jewish Americans, there continue to exist in our country people who will sell their consciences and they propose to buy these people out with their dollars, in order to further their aims.

The fact that the Greek Prime Minister took the decision to change the heads of Public Organisations and the people in their close circle, shows how much he is afraid of even the partial disintegration which exists in his party and government circles and how much he is surrounded by the known sellers of consciences.

It was written in the press favourable to the government, that Papandreou, with the way he recently acted politically intends to deliver the power to the right wing party of Mitsotakis who will undertake the responsibility to 'O.K.' the American military bases.

This is a thought which some could find to be reasonable on first sight, together with the rumour that Pandreou's intention is to instal himself as President.

When, though, you study the latest developments and combine them with the few things to which I have referred above, but chiefly when you take into consideration the past history of Andreas and his struggle on this national problem, also the positive reassurances which he had made as chief of the opposition and as Prime Minister and President of PASOK, it is difficult to believe it. That would be the worst case of Pilate-like compromise and is far worse then clearly saying 'I made a mistake and I accept that the military bases stay'.

This 'manipulation' and this 'idea' which was cleverly made public, is a creation of the CIA and of Americans who are directly interested in the matter, and I believe that they intend further action against the Greek socialist leader, because he has shown, by his stand on the bases, that he intends to lead PASOK towards International Socialism, the presidency of which he will possible undertake after Willy Brandt leaves, as has already been said.

Andreas Papandreou lived for maybe twenty years in the U.S., he acquired an American passport, he served in the American Navy, he cooperated with Americans and Jews, he married an American, his children have American citizenship, but all of this, and many other things of which he has been accused by former associates, is not enough to make him commit any national crime, because in his veins there flows Greek blood. Above and beyond this, he is a clever man. He is a man who knows, and he has been warned, that he may die violently. If he does not succumb to the demands he may (though less likely of course) be the victim of a 'crazy' assassin, because lunatics still exist.

As a clever man, though, he will prefer to die as a hero and patriot and not as a traitor.

I have said all this a little bit clumsily but I have to do it, because I believe that 'you can't handcuff conscience' and because I believe that Kazantzakis is right when he says: 'Grace to him who before others shut his mouth with soil, forestalls them and says just one syllable of his own'.

This is my own 'syllable', and this I believe and hope to be that of Greece and above all that of Andreas Papandreou.

Photograph taken during Willy Brandt's visit in Athens. From left: Vassos Mathiopoulos, author of the preface of this book, the Dean of the School of Political Science, the Speaker of the Greek Parliament Mr Yannis Alevras and Mr. George Papandreou, a deputy of the Socialist party.

Vassos P. Mathiopoulos

Vassos P. Mathiopoulos, who wrote the preface, is a Greek journalist, publicist, historian and author of a number of books.

He is well known in Greece and abroad, especially in Germany, for his activities during the military dictatorship of 1967–1974, in particular for his role as a Deutsche Welle broadcaster leading the campaign for the restoration of democracy in Greece.

Mathiopoulos, a personal friend and collaborator of Willy Brandt, is currently General Director of the Information Service of the Greek Foreign Ministry.

140

The Greek Prime Minister Mr. Andreas Papandreou, with President Willy Brandt, during Willy Brandt's last visit in Athens.

The State Department and the CIA are systematically spying on and keeping files of all Socialist leaders. Irrefutable proof is offered by the confidential report of the American Foreign Minister (above), circulated among U.S. officials, on May 20, 1981, i.e. the day before the President of France Francois Mitterand took his oath of office. The French President is called among other things 'a romantic person, under-informed, ill-advised, with literary tendencies and murky goals'.

Christian *SOURIS*   Jacques *OFFERGELD*

C.C.C., tueurs du Brabant, la Belgique, pays traditionnellement paisible et tranquille, se trouve confrontée à une vaste opération de déstabilisation sanglante.

Deux journalistes ont enquêté !

La situation actuelle n'est pas due au hasard, mais bien à l'incompétence des pouvoirs publics et à une opération internationale.

Les ramifications découvertes conduisent de Bruxelles à Tripoli, de Liège à Bucarest, d'Anvers au Liban. Si l'Europe des technocrates se traîne, celle des terroristes

The authors of the disgraceful Belgian book, slandering the Greek Prime Minister Mr. Andreas Papandreou, Christian Souris (left) and Jacques Offergeld, the first of Greek and the second of Jewish origin, both Belgian citizens.

Another photograph taken during the visit of the President of the Socialist International in Athens, where he was honoured by the School of Political Science. From left: Willy Brandt, the Minister of the Interior, Mr Akis Tzochatzopoulos, the Dean of the School of Political Science, Mr P. Kontogiorgis and the socialist member of Parliament Mr George Papandreou.

This book by Manos Haris was published by PICTON PUBLISHING of Great Britain and printed by PICTON PRINT in July 1988 to be circulated in Great Britain, U.S.A., Canada and Australia.